FOUL DEEDS AND SUSPICIOUS
DEATHS IN AND AROUND SHEFFIELD

TRUE CRIME FROM WHARNCLIFFE

Foul Deeds and Suspicious Deaths Series

Barking, Dagenham & Chadwell Heath
Barnsley
Bath
Bedford
Birmingham
Black Country
Blackburn and Hyndburn
Bolton
Bradford
Brighton
Bristol
Cambridge
Carlisle
Chesterfield
Colchester
Coventry
Croydon
Derby
Dublin
Durham
Ealing
Folkestone and Dover
Grimsby
Guernsey
Guildford
Halifax
Hampstead, Holborn and St Pancras
Huddersfield
Hull

Leeds
Leicester
Lewisham and Deptford
Liverpool
London's East End
London's West End
Manchester
Mansfield
More Foul Deeds Birmingham
More Foul Deeds Chesterfield
More Foul Deeds Wakefield
Newcastle
Newport
Norfolk
Northampton
Nottingham
Oxfordshire
Pontefract and Castleford
Portsmouth
Rotherham
Scunthorpe
Southend-on-Sea
Staffordshire and The Potteries
Stratford and South Warwickshire
Tees
Warwickshire
Wigan
York

OTHER TRUE CRIME BOOKS FROM WHARNCLIFFE

A-Z of Yorkshire Murder
Black Barnsley
Brighton Crime and Vice 1800-2000
Durham Executions
Essex Murders
Executions & Hangings in Newcastle
    and Morpeth
Norfolk Mayhem and Murder

Norwich Murders
Strangeways Hanged
The A-Z of London Murders
Unsolved Murders in Victorian and
    Edwardian London
Unsolved Norfolk Murders
Unsolved Yorkshire Murders
Yorkshire's Murderous Women

Please contact us via any of the methods below for more information or a catalogue.

WHARNCLIFFE BOOKS

47 Church Street – Barnsley – South Yorkshire – S70 2AS
Tel: 01226 734555 – 734222 Fax: 01226 – 734438
E-mail: enquiries@pen-and-sword.co.uk
Website: www.wharncliffebooks.co.uk

Foul Deeds & Suspicious Deaths in and around

SHEFFIELD

GEOFFREY HOWSE

This book is dedicated to
ANN HOWSE
& in fondest memory of
JOSEPH HOWSE

First published in Great Britain in 2009 by
Wharncliffe Local History
an imprint of
Pen & Sword Books Ltd
47 Church Street
Barnsley
South Yorkshire
S70 2AS

ISBN 978 1 84563 108 6

A CIP catalogue record for this book is available from the British Library.

Typeset in 11/13pt Plantin by
Mac Style, Beverley, East Yorkshire

Printed and bound in the UK by
the MPG Books Group

Pen & Sword Books Ltd incorporates the imprints of Pen & Sword
Aviation, Pen & Sword Maritime, Pen & Sword Military, Wharncliffe Local
History, Pen and Sword Select, Pen and Sword Military Classics and
Leo Cooper.

For a complete list of Pen & Sword titles please contact
PEN & SWORD BOOKS LIMITED
47 Church Street, Barnsley, South Yorkshire, S70 2AS, England
E-mail: enquiries@pen-and-sword.co.uk
Website: www.pen-and-sword.co.uk

Contents

Banner Cross Terrace and the Banner Cross Hotel. *Charles Peaces shot Arthur Dyson here on 29 November 1876.* The author

Introduction

To rue crime, foul deeds and sinister goings on seem to hold a fascination for a large number of people. This is my sixth book involving true crime as well as being my seventh book about Sheffield and its surrounding area. My first four true crime books concerned crimes within London, two of which were in this series, my fifth was *Foul Deeds & Suspicious Deaths in & Around Barnsley*. A second Barnsley volume is in preparation and will be followed by a South Yorkshire book in this series. For this book I have selected a wide cross-section of crimes and events surrounding the darker side of man's existence in and around Sheffield from the middle of the eighteenth century until the early 1920s.

There is so much source material concerning crime to scrutinize that from the veritable feast one is offered, it is often extremely difficult to select what to use. I am most grateful to Brian Elliott who very kindly handed over the assignment to me, along with a considerable amount of research material. I have added to this and included a varied array of not only the most heinous of crimes but also some quirky incidents. When simply to be poor was almost a crime in itself in the eyes of some, I have found it difficult to decide where the foul deed lies, particularly when one considers the harsh penalties that were meted out for comparatively trivial crimes – or indeed mere misdemeanours.

At several stages during its rich and varied history, Sheffield, like many other places in England, experienced periods of both prosperity and hardship. When leaner times came, they were more often than not felt most severely by small tradesmen, artisans and the labouring classes. Such times often resulted in an increase in criminal acts. Some unscrupulous individuals took to stealing from others to enable them to continue to live an accustomed (or indeed

A view of central Sheffield in the late Victorian period. High Street, seen here in 1892. David J Richardson Collection

enhanced) lifestyle, while no longer having to work for a living. Prolonged shortages, starvation, unemployment and a general lack of money, to buy even the essentials of life, or sometimes just the fear of that possibility or eventuality, could induce some individuals to take their own lives. The closing years of Queen Victoria's reign saw some hard times for many Sheffielders. I have selected suicides from just one year, 1892, to include in a chapter comprising eighteen cases, which is only a smattering of the suicides that occurred in and around Sheffield that year. There is also an attempted murder and suicide, which also occurred in 1892, which appears in a separate chapter, The Bath Street Shooting Case.

In my efforts to present an interesting account of each case presented here, during my research I have made every effort to cross-reference my source material. I apologise unreservedly for any errors or omissions.

Acknowledgements

I am particularly grateful to John D Murray who has assisted me over several years; and to Keith Atack, Vera Atack, Iris Ackroyd, Michael Barber, Susan Barber, Joan Bostwick, Norma Braddick, Cherrie Conlon, Robert (Bob) A Dale, Kathleen Dale, Iris J Deller, Joanna C Murray Deller, Ricky S Deller, Tracy P Deller, Brian Elliott, Doreen Howse, Joy Howse, Kathleen Howse, Dr Hidayat Hussein, Brenden E McNally, Raymond Mellor-Jones, Pamela Mott, Eleanor Nelder, Stanley Nelder, Anthony Richards, David J Richardson, Helen Vodden, Katie Vollans, Adam R Walker, Anna Walker, Christine Walker, David Walker, Emma C Walker, Ivan P Walker, Suki B Walker, Kate Ward, Helen Weatherburn, Clifford Willoughby, Margaret Willoughby, the staff of Barnsley Central Library, Doug Hindmarch, Senior Local Studies Librarian at Sheffield Central Library and the staff at Sheffield Central Library, the staff of the British Library and the staff of the British Library Newspaper Archive at Colindale.

The Stag, *formerly the* Stag Hotel, *Sharrow Head, where the resumed inquest on Arthur Dyson was held.* The author

CHAPTER 1

Meting Out of Justice in Sheffield

I n 1699, a local builder was paid £2 3s. to prepare plans for Sheffield's first Town Hall. His designs were approved and he was paid a further £200 to construct the building, which opened in 1700. The Town Hall was built on land in the south-east corner of St Peter's churchyard. St Peter's was then Sheffield's parish church and remained so until 1914, when this ancient church was raised to cathedral status; and is presently known as the Cathedral Church of St Peter and St Paul. The Town Hall was erected by the Town Trustees as a meeting place and courthouse. It was a two-storey structure, built of brick, with a pitched roof and a tower sited at the building's centre, with a belfry surmounted by a pyramidal roof, crowned with a gilded

Sheffield Parish Church, St Peter's, seen here c.1895. It was in the SE corner of St Peter's churchyard that Sheffield's first town hall stood from 1700–1810 and from where justice was administered from 1700–1808. Author's collection

ball. The hall on the first floor served as a courtroom. This courtroom was generally used for petty sessions, presided over by magistrates, but every third year the West Riding Quarter Sessions sat there. Several shops occupied space on the ground floor of the High Street side of the building, behind which a narrow passageway led to three cells, in which prisoners were kept prior to their appearance before the magistrates.

In keeping with the widely held practice throughout England, Sheffield's magistrates could only dispense justice for petty crimes. They did not have the power to try felony (crimes regarded by the law as being grave, weighty enough to be considered serious or threatening, from larceny [the illegal taking away, or stealing of another person's goods with the intention of converting them to one's own use] to more serious crimes, virtually all of which (amounting to around 200 different offences) were capital crimes. In such cases they had only the power to examine the prisoners brought before them and to decide if there was sufficient evidence to bring a charge or charges; or, if sufficiently serious, to be sent to trial at the county Assizes. Magistrates dealt with petty crime, up to and including petty larceny (taking away goods of a value of less than 12*d.* one shilling – or in today's money 5p). The stealing of goods over this value was a capital offence. Those committed for trial were usually sent to the county gaol, as bail was seldom given, and never in the case of those accused of capital offences. As Sheffield's population grew, so did the number of cases being heard before the magistrates. By 1790s the courtroom facilities at the Town Hall were inadequate for the needs of the rapidly growing town, so it became necessary for some cases to be heard in a ground-floor room at the Cutler's Hall, which served as an overspill court.

For cases involving homicide, hearings were heard before both the magistrate and the coroner. The purpose of the coroner's inquest was to establish the identity of the deceased person and the cause of death. Inquests were commonly held in public houses, usually conveniently close to where a fatality had taken place. In 1884, a public mortuary and coroner's court was built in Plum Lane and afterwards most inquests in the Sheffield district were held there. This building was replaced in 1914 by a new building in Nursery Street. Since 1977 Sheffield inquests have been held at the Medico Legal Centre in Watery Lane.

If the accused person was present at the hearing, he or she, was allowed to give evidence and to put questions to witnesses. If the coroner's jury returned a verdict of either manslaughter or murder, the coroner would then commit the prisoner to trial. This also applied in the case of prisoners already committed to trial by the magistrate. At the end of each day's court proceedings those prisoners sentenced by the magistrates to prison sentences, or to be detained in custody to await trial at the West Riding Quarter Sessions, were chained together and handed over to the custody of the town beadle. They were then taken to the Wakefield House of Correction or to the county gaol at York. In 1864, Leeds became the Assize Town for the West Riding of Yorkshire. From then onwards Sheffield's criminals would no longer be tried at York, which afterwards tried crimes committed only in the North and East Ridings.

Waingate, seen here in 2003. On the right can be seen the Town Hall, which opened in 1808 and grew in stages. Its distinctive clock tower was added in 1866. The building was reconstructed and extended between 1896–97. It provided court facilities from its opening until the 1990s. Keith Atack

By the turn of the nineteenth century, pressure had been mounting for over twenty years to replace Sheffield's first Town Hall with a more fitting structure, as the old building was deemed to be incapable of improvement. A new building fronting Castle Street, with five bays sited at the corner of Castle Street and Waingate was constructed to the designs of Charles Watson at a cost of £5,600 and opened in 1808. The old Town Hall was demolished in 1810. The new building was to serve for most of the remainder of the nineteenth century as both a magistrates' and Quarter Sessions courthouse. It contained two courtrooms, as well as four cells and offices. When Elizabeth Fry (the renowned prison reformer) visited Sheffield in 1818, the cells were already in 'a state of very great filth'. Further expansion in Sheffield resulted in the Town Hall being extended in 1833 by William Flockton. In the 1862 *Guide to Sheffield and its Neighbourhood* by Pawson and Brailsford, facilities for the prisoners had hardly improved as it states 'The Town Hall cells are confined partly underground and most unhealthy.' Flockton carried out further improvements in 1866 with his partner John L Abbot, when a central clock tower was added and the entrance was reoriented to Waingate. At the same time an underground passage was constructed to link the building to Sheffield's police offices.

In 1867, Sheffield's town councillors promoted a Bill to make Sheffield an Assize Town, with the intention of serving the southern part of the West Riding. At that time Sheffield didn't even possess a court of Quarter Sessions, and in the outlying towns and districts which under the Bill they would be required to pay part of the cost of both building a new court and administering the Assizes, there was much opposition, which eventually resulted in its withdrawal. Sheffield was granted its own Quarter Sessions in 1884 but it had to wait until 1955 to finally become an Assize town.

On Thursday 15 September 1892, the following article appeared in the *Sheffield And Rotherham Independent*:

It is a singular coincidence that a series of exhibitions of instruments of torture and death and a series of lectures on executions by an ex-executioner should be simultaneously appealing for the support of the public of Sheffield. Yet each is the case, and the circumstances suggests the idea that the two 'entertainments' might appropriately be amalgamated. Mr James Berry's lecture, and the description he gives of the methods by which capital offenders are 'worked off' at the present time, if given in the presence of the collection of cruel instruments on view in the Montgomery Hall, would afford a very powerful illustration of the growth of a humane and kindly spirit in the world towards breakers of the law as compared with the fiendish instincts which animated those who administered justice three or four centuries ago. In olden times the criminal was only allowed to die after he had undergone a protracted course of agonising torture. Now the worst of all our criminals, according to Mr Berry, is launched into eternity in less time than it takes to blow out a candle, and he has only time to feel a momentary sensation of pain.

Mr James Berry, who recently retired from the office of public executioner in Great Britain and Ireland, delivered his illustrated lecture in the Temperance Hall last night to a small audience. Mr. Berry is a young man of determined, but not unpleasant countenance. He is not a man that a child would instinctively flee from, and when he dons his tall hat and best suit he might readily be taken for a commercial traveller, as he more than once was whilst undertaking his professional journeys to various towns. Mr. Berry's lecture was characterised by good taste on the whole. Although not a polished orator, the audience would experience no difficulty in grasping the sentiments and ideas which he expressed – sometimes in very forcible language – with regard to officialism in connection with executions, and to the system of capital punishment. He explained that he voluntarily gave up his gruesome office on account of his constant disagreements with the Home Secretary and some of the Sheriffs, and which he is of [the] opinion, would ultimately [have] led to his superserssion [sic] by another and more acceptable hangman. He complains that several Sheriffs, advised by prison surgeons, tried to interfere with him in such matters as the length of the drop. He greatly prides himself on his methods of carrying out the extreme penalty of the law, and boasts that of the 150 executions he has conducted not one has been attended with the slightest mishap. The decapitation of Conway [John Conway, hanged by Berry at Kirkdale Prison on 10 August 1891] *at Liverpool, he says, was the result of interference .He wanted a drop less than four feet, the surgeon advised a six foot drop, the Sheriff supported the doctor, and he had his way, with the result which is known. The lecturer incidentally remarked that he had made up his mind that, in the event of an accident occurring, he would refuse to go down into the pit and attend to the criminal – his nerve would forsake him in such an ordeal. He also asserted that he lost favour with the Home Secretary for openly expressing his disgust with some of the decisions of that Minister on memorials praying for reprieves. He was particularly severe with the Home Secretary, and he advocated the abolition of capital punishment, for one reason because the present system places the power of granting life and death entirely in the hands of one man. His experience also leads him to the opinion that capital punishment does not act as a deterrent, but that it is feared less than penal servitude and the cat* [the multi-stranded leather whip with ferocious tips, with which criminals were punished, more commonly known as the 'cat o' nine tails'. The severity of this punishment sometimes resulted in death if a sufficient number of strokes were administered at one time, or, more often than not, death was the result of infection of the wounds sustained.] *Another argument used was that it is possible for innocent people to be hanged. He insinuated that Roman Catholics had been more leniently treated than Protestants, and that it was usual to bring in as of unsound mind criminals with genteel connections.*

The lecturer related the circumstances of the execution of three men, one of whom named Baker, told him that he shot an inspector at Romford, in Essex, whereas one of his pals, named Lee, was hanged for the crime [Anthony Rudge, John Martin and James Baker, were hanged at Carlisle on 8 February 1886 for the murder of PC Bymes. James Lee, aged forty-five was hanged at Chelmsford on 18 May 1885]. *He* [Berry] *remembered Lee cursing and swearing at the judges and lawyers for sentencing him to death, and denying the crime. All four however, were dreadful criminals and deserved death. He frequently executed men who were clearly insane, and never failed to complain about it. A man at Lancaster was so mad that he bit into him and a warder, and had to be carried to the scaffold by the frog's march. On the other hand, he had seen a reprieve come to a condemned man as he was writing out his confession. It was a case where there was some doubt as to the man's guilt. He* [Berry] *was in the cell the night before the execution was to take place, and saw him writing the confession. When the governor told him that the reprieve had come he* [Berry] *related what he had seen, the circumstance was telegraphed to the Home Secretary, who refused to withdraw the reprieve. When the boy Davis was hanged at Crewe for murdering his father he said the governor of Knutsford Prison went nearly mad, he was so disgusted at the Home Secretary's refusal to reprieve him* [Richard Davis was hanged on 8 April 1890]. *He also had to hang a boy of 17 in the South of England, who spent the eve of his death crying for his mother. When he had to execute the brothers Boswell, at Worcester, for shooting a gamekeeper, he allowed them to kiss one another and shake hands as they stood on the scaffold. They denied their guilt, and their companion stated that he, and no one else fired the fatal shot* [Joseph and Samuel Boswell, aged twenty-nine and thirty-nine respectively, were executed on 11 March 1890]. *The lecturer stated that he got in the company of a number of jurymen one evening during the sitting of an Assize, to whom he explained his views on the question of capital punishment, and his belief that murder was rarely committed by sane people, and the result of his conversation was that none of the four men on trial for murder were hanged. He said he was writing a letter which he hoped to get into the hands of the Queen, urging her to make her reign memorable by refusing to sign any more death warrants. He also wants a Royal Commission of inquiry into the circumstances under which reprieves have been granted or withheld. – We learned that Mr Berry received £10 for every execution, in addition to his expenses. His lecture will be continued all the week.*

By the 1890s work was underway to build Sheffield an even grander Town Hall, this time without the provision of court facilities. This new building was constructed between 1891 and 1896, in Pinstone Street, to the designs of E W Mountford, at a cost of £80,000. It was officially opened by Queen Victoria on 21 May 1897. The Old Town Hall in Waingate was reconstructed and extended between 1896–7 to house Sheffield County Court and Sheffield High Court. These courts remained there until they moved to new premises in the 1990s.

Sheffield Town Hall. This most recent of Sheffield's town halls is seen here shortly after its official opening by Queen Victoria in May 1897. Author's collection

An 1830s view of Sheffield, which grew on seven hills and had five rivers running through its valleys: the Don, Sheaf (from which Sheffield took its name), Loxley, Porter and Rivelin. Seen here, before heavy industry and the building of new housing to accommodate the town's rapidly growing population completely changed the landscape. Author's collection

CHAPTER 2

Foul Deeds from 1766–1923

Caught Stealing in Sheffield Market Place, 1766

… driven through the City of York on a cart …

In the spring of 1766 Caleb Roberts and Matthew Lambert, both linen drapers, were residents in Sheffield Market Place. Whilst they were hard at work another Sheffield resident, one Isaac Turner, was also being industrious in their homes, stealing their goods and possessions. Caught in the act, he was brought before Sheffield magistrates charged with theft and subsequently arraigned to appear before Mr Justice Bathurst at York Lent Assizes. Found guilty as charged, Turner was sentenced to death. On Saturday 6 March 1766, Isaac Turner was removed from the condemned cell and, along with two other felons, driven through the City of York on a cart and hanged at Tyburn.

Ex-Apprentice Recognised During Robbery, 1775

… a gang of villains whose speciality was to rob the patrons of Sheffield's public houses, hotels and inns …

John Vickers was born at Hemsworth Back Moor in Norton. Later on in life he moved to Attercliffe. As a young man there he became involved with some of Sheffield and district's more unsavoury residents, joining a gang of villains whose speciality was to rob the patrons of Sheffield's public houses, hotels and inns, who often emerged from those establishments the worse for strong drink. Such vulnerable prey often yielded rich pickings for the likes of John Vickers. Vickers, however, was to come to a sticky end in 1775, when he unwittingly selected the wrong person to rob. The victim of what proved to be Vickers' last robbery turned out to be a man to whom he was once apprenticed. The victim of this robbery, John Stainforth, having recognised Vickers during the attack on him, brought him quickly to the attention of the authorities. This led to Vickers' apprehension and to him being charged not only with robbing Mr Stainforth but also John Murfin, along with his alleged accomplice.

The events leading up to Vickers' downfall began on the night of Saturday 11 February 1775. Vickers was up to no good with one of his accomplices, John Booth and several unknown individuals. Sometime between 11pm and midnight, Vickers and John Booth allegedly robbed John Murfin of 3½d., a bad shilling, a breast of mutton and half a pound of butter. This robbery took place near the *Blue Ball*. On the same night Vickers and three persons unknown and unidentifiable to the victim, robbed John Stainforth outside the *Glass House* of 3s.6d., a leg of mutton, 6lb of sugar, some flax and small sundry items.

Vickers was brought before Mr Justice Gould at York Summer Assizes on two charges of robbery. He was indicted with Booth on the first charge for robbing John Murfin. Booth was acquitted of the charge of robbing Mr Murfin but Vickers was found guilty and sentenced to death. He was hanged at York's Tyburn on Saturday 30 March 1775.

Sheffield Button Maker's House Robbed, 1786

… stole some horn combs and 7d …

On 19 August 1786, two felons were hanged at Tyburn, York for a crime they had committed in Sheffield earlier that summer. Twenty-six-year-old William Sharp hailed from Conisborough. His accomplice in crime was twenty-eight-year-old labourer, William Bamford, of Clifton, Rotherham. Sharp and Bamford's rapid journey to the scaffold began when they broke into the house of Sheffield button maker Duncan McDonald and stole some horn combs and 7d. They were apprehended for the crime and promptly brought before a magistrate who committed them to the West Riding Quarter Sessions, where they were found guilty as charged and sentenced to death.

Ultimate Penalty for Dubious Crime, 1793

... he was committed for trial at York Summer Assizes, charged with bestiality.

The term 'Blood Money' is seldom used in normal parlance these days. If we hear it at all it is usually with reference to persons receiving compensation, often in cases abroad, because someone close to them has been murdered. We might occasionally hear Blood Money mentioned in feature films or in period costume dramas on the television, but for most people exactly where the true meaning lies, is not entirely clear. In England, from the seventeenth century until at least the end of the Georgian period, several statutes dating variously throughout the seventeenth and eighteenth centuries offered a reward to those who brought a successful prosecution against a felon. The reward varied depending on the crime but it usually fell somewhere between £10 to as much as £40. Perhaps not surprisingly, when such large sums were being offered, the system was open to abuse and certain individuals devised schemes to entrap an unfortunate victim in order that they might be successfully accused and convicted of a crime by a false accusation, thereby securing the reward of Blood Money. In 1818 the fixed statutory rewards known as Blood Money, were replaced by rewards which were at a particular court's discretion.

There was a widely held belief that one such scheme was perpetrated in Sheffield in 1793 by two labourers, John Hunt and William Warburton. If this was the case, they certainly chose a highly vulnerable victim. Seventy-seven-year-old John Hoyland, of Attercliffe, was a much put upon and ill-used old man. Apparently harmless, he had brought up a large family but suffered much abuse and even violence at the hands of his sons, who apparently took their mother's side against him whenever a quarrel arose. Witnesses said the old man was often bruised and battered. Hunt and Warburton reported to the authorities that on 15 July 1793 they had seen John Hoyland copulating with an ass. As a result the old man was arrested. He denied the accusation from the outset but this was to no avail and he was committed for trial at York Summer Assizes, charged with bestiality. The jury believed his accusers and convicted him. He was sentenced to death. On Saturday 9 August, as he stood at Tyburn, York, waiting to be 'turned off', he still protested his innocence. Perhaps his belief that the justice he had received here on earth would not be forgotten in heaven, when he declared that he would not change places with John Hunt and William Warburton, the men who had 'sworn his life away'.

Baby's Body Found in River Don, Bridge Houses 1799

… that the child had been murdered was immediately evident.

Described as being a respectable looking girl in contemporary accounts, the unmarried Mary Thorpe, left her home in Ecclesfield for Sheffield in September 1799, where she took lodgings there with a widow named Hartley. She gave a false name, calling herself Ashford. Mary was heavy with child and reputedly pregnant, as she was later to remark, by a gentleman '… far above her in circumstances who had taken advantage of that elevation to tempt her on to her destruction'. In November, Mary gave birth to a boy. A week later she left her lodgings, telling her landlady she was going to stay in Derby with her sister. In fact Mary did not go to Derby. Instead she returned to Ecclesfield, although it seems not before breaking her journey to dispose of the relatively new addition to her life.

On the morning following Mary's departure from Mrs Hartley's, the body of a baby boy was found in the River Don at Bridge Houses (near The Wicker). The fact that the child had been murdered was immediately evident. The little body was discovered wrapped in a cloth. Tied round the baby's neck was a tape weighted with a heavy stone. The tape was wrapped around the neck then tightly knotted no fewer than three times. The surgeon who examined the body confirmed that the baby had been strangled. The dead child had a distinctive birthmark. When word got around concerning the discovery of the body Mrs Hartley came forward and a quick identification of the child's identity was established.

Many of Mary's friends knew that she had been pregnant when she left Ecclesfield in September and it did not escape their notice she had clearly given birth before her return. She repeatedly denied that she had given birth and went as far as to say that they were mistaken, as she hadn't even been pregnant. This threw suspicion in her direction, as her friends knew otherwise. Quickly linked to the discovery of the dead child at Bridge Houses, she was tracked down and arrested by the parish constable at her father's house. On 27 November an inquest was held before coroner John Foster. The jury brought in a verdict of murder against Mary Thorpe. The coroner committed her for trial at the next Assizes. She appeared before Mr Justice Rook on 14 March 1800 and, despite her managing to elicit a good deal of sympathy from the spectators, the jury convicted her. Mary Thorpe was hanged at Tyburn, York on Monday 17 March 1800. Afterwards her body was dissected.

Child Rapist Receives Swift Justice, 1807

… less than a week later Paramar was brought before Baron Wood at the Summer Assizes.

In Sheffield, on 21 June 1807, seventy-year-old Samuel Paramar raped a little girl under the age of ten and assaulted another child whilst attempting to rape her. Justice was swift. Less than a week later Paramar was brought before Baron Wood at the Summer Assizes. He was convicted of rape and sentenced to death. The sentence was carried out on Saturday 5 August 1807. Samuel Paramar has the dubious distinction of being the first Sheffielder to be hanged on the New Drop behind the castle at York.

Labourer Pays with his Life for his Unguarded Sexual Indiscretion, 1834

... the judge was ill at ease at being obliged to hand down the sentence the law prescribed.

Thirty-two-year-old Sheffield labourer Thomas Rodgers may have underestimated the sensibilities of his employer when he boasted to him of having committed buggery with his fellow workman, George Bennett. Judging by the events that followed this admission, buggery was not his employer's taste, as it would seem he was clearly outraged by what Rodgers had been up to and informed the authorities, resulting in Rodger's arrest. The fact that Rodgers had admitted committing buggery to his employer formed the principal case for the prosecution. When he appeared before Baron Alderson at York Spring Assizes in 1834, on being found guilty of the charge of buggery, contemporary accounts suggest the judge was ill at ease at being obliged to hand down the sentence the law prescribed.

Baron Alderson, in passing sentence of death in what onlookers described as being in a state of some distress, said:

I sincerely regret that it has fallen to my lot to pass upon you the awful sentence of the law ... the offence of which you have been convicted is one from which human nature shudders and from the contemplation of which the mind shrinks back with horror. It was one which strikes at the root of the propagation of society and is one prohibited by the laws of both God and man and you stand here convicted of having given vent to an unbridled lust, a melancholy spectacle to teach men to ask for God's holy spirit to keep their thoughts from evil.

Rodgers apparently seemed unconcerned as sentence of death was passed on him and he left the courtroom without saying a word. He was hanged along with two other men named Cook and Morrow, on Saturday 16 April 1834, before a crowd estimated to have exceeded 6,000. After his execution Thomas Rodgers was buried in the churchyard of St Mary, Castlegate, in the same grave as Cook, one of the men who had died with him.

Robbery of a Silver Watch, Bridge Street, Sheffield, December 1859

...just a short distance from his home he was violently attacked and robbed...

On 11 December 1859, Joseph White, a smith's striker, of Mill Lane, Sheffield was returning home at night. He called in for a pint of ale at the *Lord Raglan* in Bridge Street. Having finished his pint he left the public house and three men followed him out. When he was just a short distance from his home he was violently attacked and robbed of a silver watch. It later emerged that one of the men who had followed Mr White out of the *Lord Raglan* was Thomas Russell, who was later found to have had the stolen watch in his possession. On Thursday 8 March 1860, Thomas Russell appeared before Mr Justice Blackburn at York Spring Assizes. He was found guilty of robbery with violence and sentenced to four years penal servitude.

Garotte Robbery, March 1860

... he was seized from behind and held tightly by the throat.

Garotting was an assault akin to mugging, in which a thief's victim was rendered insensible by pressing on the throat with fingers or a stick. A *garrotta* was a strangling strap used in Spain for execution. This new variation on the method of execution began in England in 1851, after news came of the execution of General Lopez in Havanah by order of the Spanish Government. A detailed description of the garrotting process appeared in various English newspapers and it was not long before criminal minds were at work to adapt garrotting as a means to criminal ends.

On Saturday 11 March 1860, George Mason, alias John Smith, appeared before Mr Justice Blackburn at the Yorkshire

A contemporary engraving of the garrotte robbery attack on John Allen by George Mason and an unknown accomplice. Author's collection

Spring Assizes. He was charged with assaulting and robbing, with an unidentified accomplice, John Allen, a filesmith, of Upper Allen Street, Sheffield, on 4 January. Mr Blanchard prosecuted and Mr Foster defended. The Court heard that, on the evening of 4 January, Mr Allen had been visiting his sister at the *Royal Oak* public house. On his journey home, at about eleven o'clock, which took him by way of Hollis Croft, where he had just reached the top of the hill when he was seized from behind and held tightly by the throat. As Mr Allen experienced the sensation of some article being pressed against his windpipe, which rendered him incapable of resisting, he saw George Mason, a man who he had known for some time, come up to him. The tight hold on his throat was now causing him to feel light-headed but before unconsciousness could overtake him, he saw and felt Mason reach down and remove from his waistcoat his gold watch and silver guard chain. Mr Allen was then quickly brought back to his senses as he felt himself being hurled violently to the ground. In his dazed state Mr Allen saw Mason and a male accomplice disappear down the hill into the dark night. Fortunately Mr Allen received only minor cuts and some severe bruising. He reported the robbery to police and the following morning Mason was arrested. Mason denied any knowledge of the incident and said he was at home in bed at the time the robbery was committed. However, this statement was immediately proved false, as Mason had been seen at the head of Silver Street by one of the arresting offices after eleven o'clock, when he said he was in bed. Mason, who had previously been convicted and sentenced to penal servitude for four years, was found guilty of the assault and robbery on John Allen by the jury. Mr justice Blackburn sentenced him to be kept in penal servitude for six years.

Favourable Verdict for Would-Be Murderer, Ecclesfield, December 1860

I expect I will get seven years for this, but if I get out I will give it him if I am able.

William Crookes of Ecclesfield, a file cutter by trade, lived in a remote cottage near Smithy Wood, from where he worked. He supplemented his income as a part-time gamekeeper for Mr Jeffcock of High Hazless, an occupation he so enjoyed, and carried out with such diligence that his gamekeeping duties had somewhat overtaken his metal working activities. Crookes was an early riser and was habitually at his workbench long before dawn. At about five o'clock on the morning of 15 December 1860, he was seated working at his bench, which stood about four feet from a window, which looked out onto the road. He had a light which could be seen from outside the cottage through a gap in the external shutters, and through which a person could see what was going on inside the cottage from the road. Suddenly the sound of a gunshot was heard and a gun's contents were discharged through the window, striking Crookes in the face and shoulders, severely wounding him and causing to fall from his seat and onto the floor. On hearing the shot his wife came down the stairs and, on observing her husband's condition, lit a lamp by which to see her way and went to fetch medical help. As she hurried along the cart road she came upon a man she later identified as Joseph English, who crouched down and tried to hide his face as she hurriedly passed him. This encounter led to English's apprehension on 17 December, when a double-barrelled gun was found at his house, one barrel of which had recently been discharged. In the other barrel was some packing paper, which corresponded with that shot from the gun fired at William Crookes and found in his cottage. When charged with attempted murder English said:

I wish I had killed the bastard. I have not been out for a month.

At Yorkshire Spring Assizes, on Monday 11 March 1861, Joseph English stood in the dock charged with attempted murder. The court heard the case for the prosecution in which it was stated that English had a motive for the attack on Crookes in as much as he entertained a feeling of revenge against him, on account of Crookes having the previous September given evidence against him for trespassing in pursuit of game. The prosecution also went on to say that shortly after his arrest, on being taken before magistrates, English had commented:

I expect I will get seven years for this, but if I get out I will give it him if I am able.

The prosecution went on to say that, when taken into the receiving room at Wakefield House of Correction, English told a fellow prisoner whom he had taken into his confidence that Crookes had caused him once or twice to be taken up (arrested on game trespass offences), but he would pay for it. He told the old lag that he had tried to catch Crookes in the road but failed, so he had determined to give it to him through the window. Presumably in order to gain some form of remission, the man had passed on this intelligence top the prison authorities.

English's defence counsel, Mr Foster, made a convincing speech tearing through the prosecution's case, as if it had no foundation, sowing the seeds of doubt in the minds of the jury. Several witnesses were called to substantiate an alibi for English. Despite what was believed to be in view of the prosecution's evidence, a seemingly convincing case against English and the probability that the alibi was pure fabrication, the jury, having retired for almost an hour, returned with their verdict. Much to the surprise of the courtroom, the foreman rose and declared that the prisoner Joseph English was:

Not guilty.

English was accordingly set at liberty.

Assault Following a Married Man's Amorous Flirtations, Sheffield, April 1868

... struck him on the head with his walking stick ...

A Sheffield printing office manager named Charles Cornelius Barton brought a charge against Matthew Walker, coachman to Henry Vickers of Holmwood Lodge, for having committed what he described as a 'cowardly unprovoked and diabolical assault' on him on Sunday 29 May 1868. At Walker's subsequent appearance before magistrates at Sheffield Police Court on Saturday 4 April, the court heard that the assault consisted of Mr Barton being struck across the head by Walker with a walking stick, which Barton preferred to refer to as a 'cudgel'. The assault was not denied. However, the facts of the case proved most interesting, as the defendant put in a plea of provocation, the evidence once having been heard in court throwing an entirely different complexion on the matter.

Barton was a married man, a detail he had concealed from the defendant, his wife and their daughter to whom he proposed himself as suitor at their house. When it was discovered that Barton was a married man he was told he was not welcome at the Walker's house and Mr and Mrs Walker forbade him to see their daughter again. On Saturday 28 May, the night before the assault took place, contrary to her parent's wishes, their daughter went out with Barton to a circus. This so enraged Matthew Walker that he waited for Barton to return home the following night and struck him on the head with his walking stick, which had resulted in some blood being spilt. Barton described the attack as almost covering him in blood and 'spoiling his Sunday suit of black'.

Barton said that Miss Walker had been well aware he was a married man and he denied that the attention he had paid her could be construed into the attentions of a lover. However, a letter he had written to her was read out in court in order that the magistrates might better judge exactly what was the nature of Barton's attentions. The letter ended:

Accept my warmest love and a few thousands of kisses, and believe me to remain, – Yours very affectionately,

CHARLES

In answer to a question from the bench, Barton said that he was living with his wife, and that they lived very happily together. This prompted one of the magistrates to say to Barton that this was not likely after she became aware of his flirtations. The magistrate then went on to say that Barton must have an abundance of love if he could live with his wife and yet spare 'a few thousand kisses' for a young woman. To which Barton replied that the magistrates knew what the world was. He had lived in the great metropolis, and had seen a great deal. To which one magistrate was prompted to say Barton had seen too much. Following this exchange the bench deliberated for a few moments before their chairman told Matthew Walker that the summons should be suspended on condition that he promise not to repeat the assault.

Assault with Intent to Steal, November 1868

Robinson had been armed with a loaded pistol.

On Friday 18 December 1868, two labourers, John Robinson, aged seventeen and John Dixon, aged twenty-one, appeared before Mr Justice Brett at Leeds Assizes. They pleaded guilty to the indictment that at Sheffield on 18 November they assaulted John Rhodes with intent to steal from his person. The court heard that Robinson had been armed with a loaded pistol. The assault took place at night as Mr Rhodes was on his way home. Robinson and Dixon stopped him and a struggle ensued during which a loaded pistol went off. The judge said the circumstances of the robbery were of a bad character. The gunshot was heard by several people who came to Rhodes' aid and his two assailants were apprehended. His Lordship added:

I cannot understand why you had a pistol in your possession, but I am willing to believe that it was not pointed at the prosecutor with the intention of using it against him. As neither of you have had any charges brought against you previously, I will therefore sentence you both to fifteen month's imprisonment with hard labour.

Election Riots at Sheffield, November 1868

… Hall struck Mr Smith a violent blow on the forehead with a fish hammer.

On Wednesday 18 November 1868, the *Sheffield And Rotherham Independent* reported under the headline:

THE BOROUGH ELECTION

———

RETURN OF
HADFIELD & MUNDELLA

———

GREAT MAJORITY AND GLORIOUS
VICTORY

The members for Sheffield in the new Parliament are Mr Hadfield re-elected, Mr Mundella elected vice *and Mr Roebuck, ignominiously defeated yesterday.*

The day was a regular November day, dull and drizzling, but the heaviness of the weather was by no means reflected in the spirits of the townsfolk. Eight o'clock saw hundreds upon hundreds of men eagerly wending their way to the various polling places, with the gravity of men on a serious and solemn business. The arrangements at some of the polling booths were as bad as they could possibly be, men being kept half and three-quarters of an hour before they could record their votes. In one place a crowd was jammed for half an hour into a passage 12ft long, with two policemen at the further end to prevent their admission into a spacious room, except one at a time every three or four minutes. All this, however, was patiently borne, and the inconvenience to which the voters were put only found utterances in a few mild jokes. 'I'll give thee a glass of beer, Mester policeman, to move on,' said one man, 'I'll give thee two,' said the representative of law and order, perspiring with his efforts to keep the people back, 'to take my place.' In the centre parts of the town business proceeded as usual for an hour or two, but about eleven o'clock the gathering crowds in the streets and the growing excitement caused the more timid, or the more prudent, shopkeepers to put up their shutters ... Towards twelve o'clock a wild and semi-criminal element began to show itself. A band of young men numbering from 100 to 200, armed with sticks, brooms and rolls of bills torn off the walls, began parading the streets at a trot. After they had carried on this game for some time, they gained courage to rob, and broke into a shop in Paradise street, to steal cigars, and into the shops in Sheffield Moor, and other places. Their numbers grew from time to time, and the rapid closing of the shops showed that danger was expected. A clog shop in Sheffield Moor was very quickly divested of a number of clogs which were hanging outside. In Bowling Green street some windows were broken. The stock of fish in the shop of Mr Langley, Gibraltar Street, was promptly confiscated, and the fish were stuck on sticks and poles and carried off in triumph; the unhappy shopkeeper was pelted with mud. Outside the shop of Mr Joseph Epworth, in Meadow street, there was an iron rail, from which about half a dozen hats and hat-boxes were suspended. This temptation was too much for the self-denial of the mob, and very shortly the iron rail was pulled down and the hats were tossed about from one to another. When they had satisfied themselves with the pleasures of tossing the crownless, and in many cases brimless' hats about, this enterprising band of ragamuffins proceeded up Scotland street, where they soon attacked another fish shop. Mrs White, the proprietress, however, was not so easily to be deprived of her goods, and upon seeing the designs of the mob, she took her stand on the edge of the pavement, and by quietly rolling up her sleeves pretty plainly intimated what were her intentions. These were soon carried unto effect on the person of an enterprising youth, who emboldened by previous successes, managed to get within half a yard of the enraged fishwife, and the result was an energetic blow on the nasal organ, and the bold youth was rolling in the mud. The mob then moved off to a fruiterer's shop across the way, and soon apples and nuts were rolling by scores down the street. The band then proceeded down Scotland street, at the bottom of which they became embroiled in a row with some Irishmen, and a fight ensued, in which the Irish obtained an easy victory. As the time drew on for the closing of the poll, excited crowds thronged the central streets, and he who got a hundred yards without losing his hat had reason to believe himself born under a lucky star. There was, however, no rioting; the wild spirits in the crowd being content with a general crusade against all hats, whether respectable or otherwise ... Soon after dusk the crowd became very much quieter than could have been anticipated an hour or two before, and no damage would have been done had it not been for a gang of young roughs who amused themselves by making a tour of Fargate, Barker [sic] pool, Broomhall street, and some other streets, and smashing a number of windows on their way. Amongst the buildings to which they paid their attention was the Water Company's Office, nearly all of the windows on the first story [sic] were broken. Windows were also broken at the top of Broomhall street, in Hanover street, near the new church; and in other parts of the town. The gang were not content with simply smashing windows, but in one or two instances they made free with the content of shops. In Barker pool, they tore down one of the shutters occupied by Mr White, eating-house keeper, then smashed several of the windows, and took at all that was in reach ... Between nine and ten o'clock the streets resumed very much their wonted appearance ... It is generally admitted that the election had passed off more quietly than many previous ones ...

On Saturday 19 December, three Sheffield men appeared before Mr Justice Brett at Leeds Assizes in connection with offences committed during the election riots in Sheffield the previous month. Thomas Moore, aged twenty-eight, blade striker, Robert Morton, aged twenty-one, cutler, and Norman Hall, aged forty-one, blade forger, were indicted for '...feloniously and violently assaulting with sticks and bludgeons John Smith and stealing from his person a gold-plated Albert watchguard; also stealing from the dwelling house of the said John Smith the sum of £5 in money; and also putting him in bodily fear by reason of threats and menaces, at Sheffield on the 17th November.' Mr Barker prosecuted and Mr Blackburn defended.

Mr Barker told the court that on 17 November, the day of the election, between four and five o'clock in the afternoon, a mob armed with sticks were about the streets of Sheffield. Several of these men, including the three prisoners, ran into the *Wharncliffe Arms*, kept by John Smith and situated at 40 West Street, and demanded beer should be given to them. Mr Smith refused to give them any, so they set about smashing pictures and broke the chandelier. Some of the men then left but a few of them returned after several minutes to inflict further damage. The prisoner Hall, struck Mr Smith over the head with a piece of wood, knocking him to the ground. Once Mr Smith had fallen, the prisoner Morton went through his pockets, whilst Moore and Hall bent over him. Mr Smith struggled to the ground as the three men jostled him to the far end of the passage, all the way aiming blows at him. Then Hall struck Mr Smith a violent blow on the forehead with a fish hammer. The three men then pulled down the counter and after they had left the inn, it was discovered that between £5 and £6 had been taken from the till.

In defence, Mr Blackman said that the question really for the jury to decide was whether the accused had gone into the *Wharncliffe Arms* with the intention of stealing. He contended there was no evidence to prove that the prisoners had any such intention. He called a female witness, who stated as soon as the prisoners entered the inn the landlord, John Smith, struck Moore over the head with a poker. At this juncture it was necessary for the judge to familiarise the jury with a point of law, as it transpired that an error had occurred in the indictment. On the calendar the men were charged with assault and robbery and the case was opened as such. Mr Justice Brett pointed out to the jury that the only charge in the indictment before him was that of robbery and no matter how disgraceful the riot was in which the three accused men took part, and no matter how unjustifiable the assault they might have committed on Mr Smith, unless they believed the prisoners actually stole Mr Smith's property, then they must acquit them. However, it appears that the jury, having already heard the full particulars of the case, were not inclined to give the prisoners the benefit of doubt regarding the only offence which they now had to decide upon, and found all three guilty. In sentencing Moore, Morton and Hall to twelve months' imprisonment for robbery, his Lordship commented upon the aggravated nature of the offence.

At the same hearing, Edward Gillett, a twenty-one-year-old spring knife grinder was also found guilty of stealing property during the election riots on 17 November. He was sent to prison for six months for breaking into the shop of James Towler with several other unidentified men, and stealing, amongst other sundry items, three pounds in weight of cigars.

Rape at a Sheffield Beerhouse, January 1869

… it is impossible to deal with your case except with the utmost severity.

Twenty-six-year-old Sheffield beerhouse keeper, George Harrison employed a domestic servant, sixteen-year-old, Phoebe Winsell. In January 1869 Phoebe accused Harrison of raping her and he was arrested and charged. He subsequently appeared before Sheffield magistrates, who committed him for trial at the West Riding Assizes. On Saturday 27 March, Harrison came up for trial before Baron Cleasby. Mr Waddy appeared for the prosecution and Mr Vernon Blackburn defended. The court heard that during his wife's absence Harrison had been quick to take advantage of the young servant girl in a most lascivious and lewd manner. The defence argued that the charge which had been preferred against Harrison had been trumped up by the young woman in order to shield herself from the consequences of her own misconduct with her sweetheart. Witnesses were called who stated that they had seen Phoebe Winsell and her sweetheart under somewhat suspicious circumstances. The jury having deliberated for only a few minutes returned and delivered their verdict. Much to his astonishment, they found Harrison guilty. On hearing the verdict Harrison leaned his head on the rails in the dock. He remained with his head resting there until the Clerk of Arraigns asked him if there was anything he wished to say why sentence should not be passed upon him. Harrison replied:

> *I am innocent. I did not rape this girl. I have always lived on the most affectionate terms with my wife.*

In passing sentence the judge told Harrison:

> *You have been convicted of this rape and I really think it is one of the worst cases that has ever occurred. Here is a young woman, almost a child, going into your service as a domestic servant. Did it never occur to you that it was your duty to protect her! It was your duty to do so, and yet the first opportunity you had of your wife's absence, and that on the Sunday, you made use of, she being like a child in the hands of a man, to ruin her. It is not a subject to dwell upon, but it is impossible to deal with your case except with the utmost severity. The sentence I shall pass on you is that you be kept in penal servitude for ten years.*

Harrison once again rested his head on the rails whilst sentence was being passed, seemingly incredulous at the verdict. He was led away in what onlookers described as a stunned condition.

Shop Robberies and Burglary, March 1869

> *… during that two-week period virtually every shop in the area had been visited by this pair of cheeky thieves with varying degrees of success…*

Crookes, seen here in 1906, where a series of shop robberies were perpetrated just a few decades before. Doreen Howse Collection

For a fortnight during March 1869 the Sheffield suburbs of Walkley and Crookes Moor were subjected to a series of shop raids by two young villains, who were described as being half criminal, half mischievous. These raids had apparently been well organised and systematically planned. The grocery shop owned by William Kay, in Cundy Street, Walkley, was visited by these thieves at dusk. They bided their time until there were no other customers in the shop, somehow managed to enter the premises without ringing the bell, and took down a ham from a hook. Mrs Kay, who was in another part of the shop, was alerted by the men stumbling over something as they attempted to leave. On going into the shop she was met by one of the men, who inquired the price of certain articles. He left the shop without purchasing anything and was shortly joined in the street by his companion. When the men were gone Mrs Kay noticed almost immediately that the ham was missing. She discovered it concealed behind the counter, where it had been put as she had entered the shop. Clearly on this occasion there had been insufficient time for one of the thieves to secrete such a large item about their person before they had been disturbed. Shortly afterwards the men were in Burgoyne Road, where they visited a small spice shop owned by John Naylor. One of the men went into the shop, made a trifling purchase, and left leaving the door closed but not fastened. Within minutes the other man entered the shop undetected and removed several items, including a box of cigars from the window display. Immediately afterwards they tried a similar tactic a little further down the road at the grocery shop attached to the *Municipal Inn* kept by William Hartley, but there they abandoned their efforts when they realised they were being observed through a window between the living quarters and the shop. The men were more successful at another small shop in Walkley, where they managed to escape with a piece of bacon weighing 10lbs and a 'bladder' of lard weighing 6lbs.

Having exhausted their efforts in Walkley, the men moved on to Crookes Moor. There the thieves turned their attention to a butcher by the name of George Hodgkinson, where they varied their method slightly. One of them went to the yard door adjacent to the shop and kicked it violently. This caused a large dog that was kept in the yard to bark loudly. As the shop assistant went to investigate why the dog was barking the other man entered the shop and made off with a large ham. The following morning the two young men, apparently growing even more daring, were spotted outside the grocery shop owned by John Ward at Crookes Moor Side, where they were attempting to force the cotter pins on the shutters by means of a crowbar. Before they were able to gain entry to the shop these would-be burglars were alarmed by someone approaching and made off into the early morning mist. It transpired that during that two week period virtually every shop in the area had been visited by this pair of cheeky thieves with varying degrees of success, almost always it seems during times when the policemen on their beats were being changed.

Attempted Murder in Portland Lane, 1872

> *... Barker was at home and indulging in the common practice of thrashing his wife.*

On Tuesday 7 August 1872, forty-eight-year-old fork grinder, Edward Barker, of Portland Lane, Sheffield, appeared at

Leeds Summer Assizes before Baron Cleasby. He was indicted for 'feloniously and maliciously wounding Elizabeth Unwin at Sheffield, with intent to murder her'. A second count in the indictment charged him with 'intent to do grievous bodily harm'. Mr Barker (no relation to the prisoner) prosecuted. The prisoner was undefended.

Mr Barker outlined the background and circumstances of the case in his opening speech. He said that on the night of 29 May, Barker was at home and indulging in the common practice of thrashing his wife. Mrs Barker was lying upon the ground; her husband was kneeling upon her and had his hands in her hair. Elizabeth Unwin, a neighbour, on hearing the screams of Mrs Barker, went to see what was the matter. On finding Mrs Barker on the floor and her husband assaulting her, she caught hold of his legs, pulled him away from his wife, and begged him not to murder her. Barker immediately got up and struck Miss Unwin a heavy blow and then kicked her in the back. Miss Unwin managed to escape from her attacker, ran out of the house, and went back to her own house. Half an hour later Miss Unwin was getting her supper ready, when suddenly Edward Barker rushed into her house and stabbed her several times in the breast, back and arms, and cut her fingers. He then ran out of the house leaving Miss Unwin on the floor, almost completely covered with blood. Subsequently Barker was sitting in his house, and, when approached by a police officer, said:

See my hands are covered with blood.

A carving knife still wet with blood was found in his yard.

Mr Thorpe, the house surgeon at the Sheffield Hospital, described the nature of the wounds. In answer to a question put to him by the prisoner, Mr Thorpe said that the wounds were not sufficiently deep to be of a dangerous character. In his cross-examination of the other witnesses, the prisoner was able to establish that his wife was a drunken woman and that he had had a good deal of trouble with her. She was liable to fits, and when they were upon her, she had to be held. The witnesses, however, could not say whether Mrs Barker was having a fit on the night in question, when the attack on Miss Unwin by the prisoner had taken place. That was the case for the prosecution.

Edward Barker in his brief address to the jury said that though he had inflicted the wounds, he did not inflict them with any malice. He said that Miss Unwin had told him if he did not let his wife alone, she would send the knife into him; and it was in consequence of a quarrel which then took place, that the knife was made use of. The knife was lying on the table, she picked it up and he had inflicted the wounds in self-defence. The evidence regarding Mrs Barker's fits and Barker's contention that he had only acted in self-defence, clearly unsettled the jury. Having decided there was reasonable doubt with regard to the prisoner's intent to commit murder, taking into account the character of the wounds inflicted on Miss Unwin by the prisoner, they found him guilty of the lesser charge of intent to do grievous bodily harm. The judge in passing sentence told Barker:

The jury has found you guilty of an intention to do grievous bodily harm. They have taken a most merciful view of the case. That you should have injured Miss Unwin in the way that you did, and under so little provocation, is almost unaccountable. It is possible under the uncontrolled influence of angry feelings, you might have done more than you had intended or had thought you had done. But a man whose passions become so violent, and under the influence of which he commits such violent acts, is unfit to be at large. If the jury had found you guilty of an attempt to murder, the sentence would have been very different, but acting on their merciful verdict, I cannot pass a lighter sentence than seven years' penal servitude.

Assault in the *Union*, Carbrook 1876

… struck him several violent blows in the face …

On Friday 9 December 1876, Edward Gill, wiredrawer, of Short Street, Carbrook, appeared before the Mayor, G Bassett, Esquire and Alderman Hallam at Sheffield Town Hall, charged with assaulting steel warehouseman, Francis Curran, of Granville Street. The court heard that the assault took place on Saturday 2 December at the *Union* public house in Carbrook. On entering that establishment Gill, who was at variance with Curran concerning some disagreeable words that had sometime previously passed between them, noticed Curran and demanded an immediate apology. Curran declined to apologize so Gill struck him several violent blows in the face, knocking him down. Gill was found guilty of the assault and fined 20*s*. plus costs or the option of one month's imprisonment with hard labour.

Manslaughter in Pond Street, 1889

… he found Harriet lying on the floor completely naked, with a black eye and comatose.

On Tuesday 16 September 1890, twenty-six-year-old brickmaker, James Mitchell, appeared at Leeds Assizes before Mr Justice Smith, charged with the manslaughter of Harriet Herbert, at Sheffield on 27 October 1889. Mr Banks and Mr Edmondson acted for the prosecution. The prisoner was not represented.

Mr Banks in opening the prosecution's case said that Harriet Herbert, a single woman, lived in a house at 29 Court, Pond Street, together with two women named Olive Clayton and a Miss Morton. Miss Herbert had been in the habit of receiving visits from a man named Alan Mekin. On the morning of Saturday 25 October 1889 Miss Morton left the house and did not return until after Miss Herbert's death. Miss Herbert was seen by several witnesses during the early afternoon and appeared to be in perfectly good health. Later in the afternoon she went out with the prisoner and returned home late that night with him. Olive Clayton heard Mitchell use disgusting language to Miss Herbert in connection with the visits she had been receiving from Mekin. Sometime later, in the small hours of Sunday morning, a row was heard by neighbours between Mitchell and Miss Herbert. A man named Biggin who lived next door, heard cries of 'murder'.

These cries were also heard by a boy named Swaine, who was out playing in the court with another boy and on hearing the noise at No 29 went to the door and peeped through the keyhole, were he saw:

> *… a master kicking the missus …*

It was then suggested that what the boy saw was the prisoner inflicting the injuries on the woman that would eventually lead to her death. Miss Herbert had died from a ruptured kidney and the medical evidence showed that the rupture had been caused by kicking. Mr Banks said that Mitchell admitted that he had spent the entire night at the house, and there was no evidence to show that any other woman who was in the house had been kicked. Olive Clayton, who had been in the house on the Saturday night left on Sunday morning and kept out of the way, not returning until after Miss Herbert's death. On the previous night she had heard the voice of the other man, Mekin, in the house, downstairs, and an altercation going on. She also heard him asked by someone to 'open the door' and heard someone say 'I'm off.' That account coincided with the one provided by Mekin himself. Miss Herbert had kept company with Mekin for some time and she had a child by him. Subsequently she began seeing Mitchell. On the Saturday night in question Mekin had gone to the house quite late and had found the prisoner lying on an improvised bed in a downstairs room, and that had prompted Harriet to say to Mekin that he had found them out at last. Mekin took her outside and told her if she had only told him she had taken up with Mitchell he would not have come near her. While they were talking Mitchell came up and said: 'I'll go.' He seemed happy to do so but a short while later he returned in a violent frame of mind. He threw his coat over the candle and knocked the light out, whereupon Mekin remarked, 'if that's it I'm off' and he left the house. Mekin did not return to the house until Monday morning, when he found Harriet lying on the floor completely naked, with a black eye and comatose. He fetched a neighbour, Mrs Bradbury and she helped him carry Harriet upstairs to bed. Harriet never regained consciousness and died the following day. The Crown would ask the jury if the prisoner had inflicted those injuries, that he was the man who alone was there, and had the opportunity of doing so, and that it was those injuries that had caused her death.

Witnesses were then called. The medical evidence was provided by the surgeon who had conducted the post-mortem examination on the body, Mr Arthur Hallam. He said he found Miss Herbert had a ruptured kidney, which it was possible would have been caused by a blow, indicated by a severe bruise, which he had found on the left hip. There must have been some violence used to cause the rupture. Detective Inspector Thompson gave evidence regarding the state in which he found the deceased on the Monday and regarding the statements made by both Mekin and the prisoner. Allan Thomas Mekin, carter, said he had been keeping company with Harriet Herbert for about four years. On the Saturday night in question he had gone to the deceased's house at 11.30pm, knocked on the door and entered. He had seen Mitchell lying on the sofa and Harriet was standing against the stairs leading to the bedroom. Mekin then went on to describe the conversation which had taken place between himself and the deceased. He concluded his evidence by saying that he had left the house about 1.30am and during the time he had been there had seen no violence towards the deceased on the part of the prisoner. Several other witnesses were called and none of them threw any further light as to how the deceased had received her injuries, other than had been already suggested, as a result of her having been kicked by the prisoner. Several witnesses commented on the prisoner's use of filthy, disgusting language when he had been drinking. Witnesses evidence indicated that had been the case on the night the prisoner had allegedly kicked the deceased. Mr Hallam was recalled and asked by his Lordship if the rupture could have been caused a week or ten days before her death. In his reply the surgeon told his Lordship that he considered that from the extravasation of blood that was impossible. The utmost limit he could give would be fifty-six hours.

Mr Justice Smith in his summing up told the jury that their duty was plain. He went on to say:

You have to find out first whether the case put by the Crown that the prisoner had kicked the deceased was correct, and secondly whether the deceased came to her death as a result of those blows. The great question is whether the man kicked the woman. In this case there has been remarkable testimony given. I do not intend to offer any theory as to how that testimony has been put together...

The jury deliberated for an hour and returned with a guilty verdict. In passing sentence his Lordship told the prisoner that he concurred with the jury's verdict and he believed that Mitchell had kicked the poor woman. Mitchell was sent to prison for fifteen months with hard labour.

Brutality to a Pit Pony, 1891

... struck the pony with the pick he had in his hand.

On 14 January 1892, John William Dyson, of Park Hill, Sheffield, a miner at Woodthorpe Pit, appeared before the stipendiary magistrate at Sheffield Town Hall, charged with cruelty to a pit pony. Dyson admitted the offence. He said on 23 December 1891 he had a particularly heavy workload. The pony in his charge was behaving stupidly. He was in a temper and, forgetting what he was doing, struck the pony with the pick he had in his hand. When he saw the injury he had inflicted upon the poor animal he was mortified. He immediately took the pony to the stable to receive attention. Dyson said he was very sorry for what he had done. He was fined £2 1s. 6d.

Drunken Labourer Driven Out of House With a Table Leg, July 1892

Proderick then ran wildly about the street with blood streaming from his head.

Labourer Patrick Proderick, an inveterate drunkard, appeared before Mr Frank Mappin and Alderman Clegg, at Sheffield

Town Hall, on Tuesday 26 July 1892. The bench were told that on the previous night Proderick was drunk and disorderly in Bailey Street. He entered a private residence occupied by Mrs Hardy and promptly proceeded to assault her son. He then kicked a leg off the table. Mrs Hardy picked up the table leg and drove Proderick out of the house by striking him on the head with it. Proderick then ran wildly about the street with blood streaming from his head. He eventually came to the attention of Police Constable Jennis, who took him to the hospital, where his wounds were attended to. Afterwards he was taken to the Police Station and looked up for the night. Proderick admitted to having previously been fined for similar offences. On this occasion he was given a fine of 20*s.*, including costs.

Unmanly Son Stole From His Mother, July 1892

He admitted the theft and attempted to excuse himself by saying he was full of drink.

Mrs Jackson, a widow, lived in Marshall Street, Sheffield. Her son, Frederick, a powerfully built young man, worked as a plate-layer. He occasionally came to live with his mother, but far from assisting her in her declining years and far better placed to earn a living than she, Frederick Jackson sponged on her good nature and as soon as the opportunity presented

Sheffield's stipendiary magistrate, Edward M E Welby (1836–1926), who occupied the post from 1874–1914. News Archive

itself, stole the whole of her savings and appropriated the money to his own purposes.

On the morning of Monday 25 July 1892, Mrs Jackson went out leaving the house locked up and money in gold and silver coin amounting to £8 locked in a drawer in the bedroom. When she returned home that evening she found the doors forced open and the money missing. She informed the police, who, having made enquiries in the area, arrested her son a few hours later at about midnight. He admitted the theft and attempted to excuse himself by saying he was full of drink.

When Frederick Jackson was brought before the stipendiary magistrate at Sheffield Town Hall on Wednesday 27 July, Mrs Jackson was asked if she thought her son deserved six months in prison. To that question the prisoner's mother replied:

Yes, two six months, although I am his mother.

Jackson was given a forty-two-day prison sentence.

Labourer Dies in Street Row, July 1892

One man struck Jackson in the face while several others kicked him severely.

On Saturday 2 July 1892, twenty-year-old, labourer, Walter Jackson of 26 Carlisle Street East, Attercliffe and a friend of his, Walter Jarvis, a carter from Grimesthorpe, went into town together at about eight o'clock in the evening. They visited two public houses before visiting a third, the *George and Dragon* in Bank Street, where they were joined by Samuel Milner, who had come there from his home in Page Hall Road, Grimesthorpe. They left the *George and Dragon* at eleven o'clock and stood outside talking for twenty-five minutes. Then Jackson and Milner left Jarvis and walked up Bank Street to the top of Snig Hill, where a street row was in progress. Two men were fighting and Walter Jackson pushed his way to the front of a crowd that had assembled, to try and persuade a man he knew to come away, while at the same time his friend, Milner, entreated Jackson himself to come away and go home. A man in the crowd approached Jackson and said:

There's a man in the crowd a stone lighter than you and he'll fight you.

Jackson was not even given the opportunity to respond to this remark before the man who was allegedly a stone lighter, in readiness, had taken off his coat and immediately struck Jackson in the face. Jackson pushed his assailant away and the man fell to the ground, whereupon several of the fallen man's friends set upon Jackson. One man struck Jackson in the face while several others kicked him severely. Before any more damage could be done the police arrived and the crowd quickly dispersed. Milner left Jackson in Snig Hill and went back into Bank Street where he met up with Jarvis and informed him that Jackson had got into a row. When they arrived back in Snig Hill, Jackson was not there. They went off in opposite directions to find him and shortly afterwards Milner came upon Jackson wandering in The Wicker, where he procured some meat to put on Jackson's severely bruised eye. He assisted Jackson home, who all the while was complaining of a pain in his head and of feeling very sick and dizzy. As the two men reached Carlisle Street they were joined by Jarvis who helped get Jackson into the house, where they arrived at 12.30am. Jackson lay on the couch for an hour before retiring to bed. He refused to take all his clothes off and got into bed semi-dressed. His brother remained in the room with him until two o'clock then went to his own room to sleep. When he returned to his brother's room at nine o'clock he found that Walter was dead.

The coroner ordered a post-mortem examination, which was conducted by a surgeon, Mr Thomas Finney. An inquest opened on Wednesday 5 July before coroner Dossey Wightman, Esquire, at the *Carwood Hotel*. Mr Finney, in giving the medical evidence, said the deceased had died as a result of being struck on the head, the blow having inflicted severe internal injuries. The inquest was then adjourned until Wednesday 12 July at the same venue.

John Theodore Bell, who lived in Rittle Street, said he was employed at a tobacco shop owned by Mr Dennie in Bank Street. On the night of 2 July he was working in his master's shop, from where he saw the disturbance in Snig Hill.

Although he saw Walter Jackson being struck, he could not say which man or men assaulted him.

The coroner said that the police had been unable to ascertain the names of the man or men who had been involved in the argument. Nobody else who either witnessed or took part in the incident had come forward or been found. It was up to the jury to decide whether an open verdict should be returned, leaving the matter in the hands of the police, or whether the inquest should be further adjourned. After considerable consultation the jury returned with an open verdict. The coroner recorded that Walter Jackson had died as the result of apoplexy caused by violence inflicted by some person or persons unknown.

Bigamy, Pitsmoor, November 1892

… she told the Court that James Phoenix had been her 'first love' and that she had intended to 'settle down' with him.

In November 1892, twenty-nine-year-old Elizabeth Rogers was indicted for bigamy at Sheffield. On Friday 28 July 1893, her case came up at Leeds Summer Assizes before Mr Justice Bruce. Mr Wilson, acting for the prosecution, told the court that the prisoner had been married in April 1886. That marriage was still valid. However, in November 1892 she went through a form of marriage ceremony with James Phoenix at Christ Church, Pitsmoor. Intelligence reached the police of the bigamous marriage and Rogers was arrested. In her defence she told the court that James Phoenix had been her 'first love' and that she had intended to 'settle down' with him. She also said that Phoenix knew she was already married, a fact he denied when he was called as a witness. The jury found her guilty but with a recommendation to mercy. The judge clearly took the jury's recommendation into consideration when he handed down Rogers a sentence of six weeks' imprisonment.

Vicious Assault With a Coal Rake, 1904

… struck him repeatedly on the head with a coal rake…

Thirty-nine-year-old labourer, William Henry Bullevent appeared at Sheffield City Sessions before Assistant Recorder Mr S H C Lofthouse KC, on Friday 30 January 1904, indicted for maliciously wounding Patrick Butler on 7 November. Mr Slater appeared for the prosecution. The court heard that Mr Butler, a hawker, living at No 13 House, No 4 Court, Garden Street, went outside his house at eleven o'clock at night. Bullevent, who was standing there, without any provocation and for no apparent reason, struck him repeatedly on the head with a coal rake, causing six severe wounds, resulting in Mr Butler's hospitalisation. The prisoner interjected as evidence was being given to say that it was a stick he had used to hit him with, although witness evidence contradicted this assertion. Evidence was presented which showed that Mr Butler had no quarrel with Bullevent. The prisoner was found guilty as charged. As he had already spent two months in prison awaiting his trial, he was sentenced to an additional month.

Fraud Concerning Charitable Contributions, Chapeltown, 1905

… said he had obtained the money in order to secure food for his wife and children.

Two young moulders from Chapeltown, John Gandy and Tom Watson, appeared at Sheffield West Riding Court before Mr B J Young and Dr Dyson, on Friday 7 April 1905, charged with fraudulently obtaining charitable donations. The bench heard that Gandy and Watson went around the Chapeltown district falsely representing themselves as authorised to collect contributions on behalf of Chapeltown Central Cricket Club. Between 17–25 March they collected nine amounts ranging from 5s. to 6d. and totalling between 17s. and 18s. Once club officials became aware of Gandy and Watson's activities, they complained to the police. Detective Sergeant Denney arrested them in a public house in Sheffield. Watson, who was married, said he had obtained the money in order to secure food for his wife and children. He had no previous convictions against him and Superintendent Beilby expressed the opinion that the idea of collecting the money did not originate with him. Gandy, however, had eleven previous convictions, all but one for minor offences. The bench fined him 30s. with the option of a month's imprisonment. Watson was fined 20s. or in default fourteen days imprisonment.

Appalling Cruelty to Cats, 1914

> *… witness said it was necessary for him to cover his eyes with his hands because he could not bear to see the sight.*

What was described by those who were present in court, as an exemplary punishment, which was meted out to two boys by Sheffield magistrates Alderman Wardley and Mr W Brooks, on Thursday 15 January 1914, was an opinion generally concurred with by the wider public of Sheffield. The case in question concerned such appalling cruelty to some cats, that the sensibilities of all true animal lovers who either read or heard about the case were severely shaken. Two youths, aged thirteen and seventeen respectively, were charged with ill-treating five cats by tying them with a rope and beating them to death with an iron bar.

The bench heard a shocking tale told by a young boy who was with the defendants in an outbuilding in Burgoyne Road. He described how the elder of the two boys placed a rope round the neck of a black cat, and suspended the animal by hanging the rope from a hook in the wall. The younger boy then picked up an iron bar and made an attempt to strike the cat with it. However, his bravado failed him and he abandoned his attempt. When questioned by Mr Wing, who was defending the youngest boy, the witness said:

> *He 'funked it', when he lifted the iron he threw it down again.*

As the boy went to pick it up again, the older boy took the piece of iron out of his hand and struck the cat a violent blow on the head with it. The witness said it was necessary for him to cover his eyes with his hands because he could not bear to see the sight. Another witness stated he saw the two defendants go down a passage with a cat in a bag. He saw them return a short while later and heard the younger boy say:

We have killed the cat. Let's find another.

Several cats had been reported missing from houses in the vicinity of Burgoyne Road. Enquiries were made which led to Police Constable Simpson visiting the house of the elder of the defendants, while Police Constable Froggatt visited that of the younger. Constable Simpson was taken to an outbuilding and shown where five cats had been buried. The defendant explained that he had killed the cats the previous week by holding them with a rope and striking them. The defendant then told him he had then skinned the dead animals. The other defendant, when questioned, also admitted the cats had been killed with a piece of iron. The bench heard the defendants unearthed the carcasses and the skins of the cats, in the presence of the constables. Police Constable Froggatt said when he spoke to the younger of the two defendants, the boy said to him:

I don't care what they do to me, so long as they don't touch my mother and father.

When the elder boy was asked where he had got the idea of killing the cats, he said he had visited a slaughterhouse. This prompted the magistrate's clerk to say:

Are you thinking of being a butcher? You are an engineer, aren't you?

To which came the reply:

I have been but I'm not doing anything now.

Then came another witticism from the magistrate's clerk:

Oh I see, you are learning butchering.

Toward the end of the proceedings Alderman Wardley said:

> *I cannot recall a more painful case. It is most appalling for you lads to have inflicted such grievous cruelty on dumb animals. This case is too serious to be dealt with lightly and the bench is bound to inflict a heavy penalty.*

The eldest defendant was given a fine of £3 or one month's imprisonment, the younger was fined £2.

No Receivers, No Thieves, 1923

> *... it was due to Stevenson's cooperation on his arrest that it had been possible to recover some of the stolen property.*

On Friday 13 July 1923, Sheffield Quarter Sessions were opened at the Court House before the Recorder, Mr W J Waugh, KC and the Assistant Recorder, Mr C Milton Barber. Among the twenty cases for trial, apart from the appeals, was that of thirty-eight-year-old druggist, Charlie Stevenson. Stevenson pleaded guilty to the charge of receiving 3oz. of platinum rhodium, the property of Messrs Cammell, Laird and Co. Prosecuting, Mr John Neal, said that platinum rhodium was sometimes valued at £40 an ounce but its price fluctuated. Mr Neal also pointed out that it was due to Stevenson's cooperation on his arrest that it had been possible to recover some of the stolen property. Defending Stevenson, Mr Willoughby Jardine, said his client had never been in trouble before. At the time of the theft the stolen metal was worth £23 an ounce and that Stevenson had only received £15 out of the transaction. The Recorder said:

> *If there were no receivers of precious metals there would be no thieves. While I am loth to send a man to prison for a first offence, I am bound to mark my sense of the enormity of the offence of receiving precious metals which have been stolen in a commercial community.*

Stevenson was sentenced to six months' imprisonment with hard labour.

CHAPTER 3

Charlie Peace: The Not So Lovable Rogue and the Banner Cross Murder

1876–1879

... speaks somewhat peculiarly, as though his tongue was too large for his mouth, and is a great boaster.

Charles Peace, more often than not referred to as Charlie Peace, was considered in late Victorian England to be, with the possible exception of the unidentified and unidentifiable 'Jack the Ripper', Britain's most notorious murderer. Yet in the eyes of a large faction of the public, who lionised him, Peace

Charles Peace, disguised and tooled-up for work.
Illustrated Police News

became something of a folk hero. So much so, the legacy he left in his wake resulted in this irrepressible felon being remembered with affection, rather than despised for the foul deeds he perpetrated. Following his trial and execution, all over Victorian England parents used Peace's name as a means to bring naughty children to heel, uttering the threat, 'If you don't behave, I'll set Charlie Peace on you.' I remember when I was growing up in the 1960s a cartoon strip about his exploits being featured in *Buster*, a popular children's comic of the day, more than ninety years after he was hanged. That he is, to this day, regarded by many as a celebrity, to me, beggars belief. His effigy in the Chamber of Horrors at Madame Tussaud's was for several decades one of the most popular exhibits. How on earth this grossly ugly (both in spirit and appearance), prematurely aged in appearance, devilish little man, achieved this degree of fame, and became something of a romantic hero – and a lovable rogue – clearly deserves closer scrutiny.

Charles Peace was born in Angel Court, Sheffield on 14 May 1832. His father, one time a wild beast tamer with George Wombwell's menagerie, had settled down to work as a shoemaker and was well respected. He passed onto young Charles an interest in animals and a love of music. In early life Charles also developed a flair for the Japanese art of origami

Mrs Hannah Peace. Illustrated Police News

and became quite adept at creating artistic shapes from pieces of paper. He took a keen interest in amateur theatricals and learned to play the violin, becoming sufficiently accomplished to merit the accolade 'The Modern Paganini,' on the playbills at local concerts. He was apprenticed at a Sheffield rolling mill during which time he sustained a serious injury, when a piece of red hot steel struck him on his left leg and hand, maiming his hand and leaving him with two fingers short and a permanent limp. By the time he was twenty, Charles Peace had discovered that burglary was a far easier way of earning money than actually working for a living. Short in stature, agile as a monkey and incredibly strong, Charlie wasn't very successful at first because between 1851 and 1866 he found himself behind bars on no fewer than four occasions, being sentenced variously to one month, four, six and seven years. Peace did not confine his activities to Sheffield but moved from town to town, often around the Manchester area. In 1859 he met a widow, Mrs Hannah Ward, who had a young son named Willie. Mrs Ward fell for Peace's charms and they married, Peace becoming stepfather to little Willie. They subsequently had a daughter, Jenny. They all returned to Sheffield in 1872, when Charlie's activities around Manchester were beginning to attract too much police attention.

During his exploits Peace had sustained a fractured jaw, which thereafter left him with the unusual ability of being able to alter the features of his face by protruding his lower jaw and suffusing his face with blood; changing to such an extent that he took on the appearance of a mulatto (the child of a black and a white parent). When he wished to adopt a more permanent colouration of his skin to assume a disguise, he darkened it with walnut juice. The pliability of his facial features enabled him to assume the most convincing disguises, foxing the police and the victims of his scams on numerous occasions. By this time he had perfected his technique in burglary and was generally admired by the few members of the criminal classes who were privy to his nefarious activities. The seeds of what was to become the legend that is Charlie Peace had been sown.

In 1875, Peace went into business. He moved with Hannah, Willie and Jenny to Darnall, then still a village, situated to the east of the Sheffield, near Attercliffe. The Peaces took up residence at 40 Victoria Place, Brittania Road, where Charlie set up shop and traded as a picture framer and guilder. He also sold musical instruments and bric-a-brac. When committing burglaries, which he of course continued to do, he could not resist taking violins and other musical instruments. In fact he became an avid collector. This passion for procuring musical instruments, more often than not by purloining them, was to remain with him for the remainder of his 'career'. Next door but one to the Peaces in Victoria Place lived Mr and Mrs Dyson and their five-year-old son. Arthur Dyson was a civil engineer, who worked for the North Eastern Railway. In his early career he was in business in Sheffield and was the first surveyor appointed by the trustees under the Sheffield And Tinsley Turnpike Act. He later worked abroad. He was the son of Henry Dyson, a farmer and land valuer at Tinsley. Standing 6ft 5in tall, with good manners and genteel disposition, Arthur Dyson had met and married his Irish wife Katherine when he was in America in 1866. Seven years later they returned to England and before moving to Darnall they had lived with Dyson's mother in Tinsley.

It was not long before the Dysons became known to the Peaces, after Charlie was commissioned to frame four pictures, including one of Dyson's mother. Charlie was very taken with Kate Dyson from the start. She was a tall, buxom woman, almost twenty years younger than Charlie. She was rather too fond of strong drink and she and her husband were prone to having rows. By this time Charlie was forty-three, but looked considerably older. He had a tendency to stoop, and notwithstanding his limp was also bow-legged. Despite what one might reasonably deem to be considerable shortcomings, it appears he was something of a charmer with the ladies and, when he tried his luck, Kate Dyson responded favourably. They took to going out together and were seen at various public houses, music halls and other places of entertainment. Charlie and Kate went to Sheffield Fair. They were even photographed together. The house that stood between their two homes was empty. It was in the garret there that they were able indulge their caprices. Peace's fascination for Kate made him become something of a nuisance, at least to Arthur Dyson. He would call on the Dysons whenever he chose, sometimes even at mealtimes. This continued until Arthur Dyson told him his constant visits were not acceptable. However, her husband's refusal to welcome Charlie into the house, whenever he chose to turn up, was clearly not to Kate's liking, as she took to sending her paramour notes, informing him when Arthur would be out and not likely to return. By June 1876 Arthur Dyson had had enough of Charlie Peace. He made it quite clear that he was not welcome to call at the house any more. He wrote a note on a visiting card and threw it into Peace's yard. It read:

Charles Peace is requested not to interfere with my family.

On Saturday 1 July, Charlie Peace came upon Arthur Dyson in the street and deliberately tripped him up. That evening Charlie noticed Kate standing outside her house talking to three female neighbours. He walked up to them and demanded to know if they were talking about him. When Kate replied that they were, Charlie insisted on being told what had been said. When it emerged that she had been complaining about the assault on her husband, Peace pulled out a revolver and said in a menacing tone:

I will blow your bloody brains out and your husband's too!

The following morning a magistrate's warrant was obtained for Peace's arrest but the bird had flown. The Peace family moved temporarily to Hull, where Mrs Peace found work as a supervisor at some dining rooms. Charlie simply continued to fill the family's coffers by committing burglary at night time, whenever the opportunity presented itself, in Hull and wherever his fancy took him, and as usual he travelled extensively and even went back to Sheffield on several occasion, as his flair for adopting convincing disguises presented no barriers. He also spent some time around the Manchester area.

Arthur Dyson was relieved to discover that Peace had left the neighbourhood. He no doubt enjoyed the relatively brief respite he had had since his troublesome neighbour's disappearance. However, he evidently entertained some doubt about his wife's association with Peace and perhaps was not entirely convinced that this thorn in his side would not return. Clearly in an attempt to avoid this possibility, Arthur Dyson found his family a new home on the south-eastern edge of Sheffield in Banner Cross Terrace, off Eccleshall Road, about six miles from Darnall. Banner Cross Terrace stood on the left hand side of the road in a secluded position, the gardens at the back being overlooked by the road from Sharrow to Eccleshall. Although the terrace was some hundreds of yards from the nearest other dwellings, it was nevertheless a relatively busy place, with regular traffic in the main thoroughfare opposite and a near constant flow of passers by on foot. On 26 October, having sent their furniture on ahead in a wagon earlier in the day, they arrived at Banner Cross Terrace in the evening, when the furniture was still being unloaded. As the Dyson family approached the front door, Charlie Peace came out of the house to greet them. A heated exchange took place, which culminated in Peace telling Dyson:

You see, I am here to annoy you wherever you go.

When Dyson remonstrated with Peace and reminded him that there was still a warrant out for his arrest, Peace shrugged his shoulders and said he neither cared for the warrant nor for that matter, the police. Clearly satisfied with the upset he had caused, Peace left the dumbstruck Dysons and called in at Gregory's, a grocery shop situated next door to the Dyson's new home, and bought some tobacco. The Dysons saw nothing more of Peace for over a month.

Meanwhile, while the Dysons enjoyed yet another Peace-free period, Charlie was going about his usual business and once again found himself in the Manchester area, where Irish labourers, the Habron brothers, John, William and Frank, were employed by a nurseryman and farmer, Mr Francis Deakin, at the well-to-do suburb of Whalley Range, near Manchester. They slept in an outhouse on their employer's premises. In July 1876, following a night of revelry, Police

Peace shoots Police Constable Cock in the grounds of Mr Gratrix's former residence, at West Point, Whalley Range. Illustrated Police News

Constable Nicholas Cock had summoned two of the brothers for being drunk and disorderly; William received a fine on 27 July and the charge against John was dismissed on 1 August. Following the court hearing the brothers went to a beer house, the *Royal Oak*, where they were regular customers, to celebrate. After several pints some comments were uttered against the police by the brothers, which in view of events that followed, later became construed as threats. That night Constable Cock was on duty with Constable Beanland when they noticed a man loitering in what they considered to be a suspicious manner near the gate of a house in West Point, that until recently had been occupied by Mr Gratrix. The man was described later by a local man, Mr Simpson, as appearing elderly, with a stooping gait. The policemen separated to investigate and Cock followed the man as he entered the grounds of the house. Shortly afterwards two shots were heard and when Constable Beanland and a passer by, Mr Simpson, went to investigate, they found Constable Cock lying in the road, shot through the right breast. He died half an hour later.

Suspicion immediately fell upon the Habrons. Police were quick to call at the outhouses where they lived. They found them naked in bed and arrested all three of them. Their arrest was prompted by the police seeing a light as they arrived at the outhouses, this they said was immediately extinguished as the brothers heard their footsteps approaching, clearly evidence of their guilt. The brothers were ordered to put on the clothes they had been wearing the previous day. They were arrested and taken to Northumberland Street Police Station.

When the scene of the murder was examined the following morning, a boot print was found in the mud. This was compared with a wet muddy boot worn by John Habron and it appeared to match. Some percussion caps were found in the waistcoat worn by William Habron. Frank Habron was later released but John and William were sent for trial at Manchester Assizes on 27 November, before Mr Justice Lindley. The prosecution maintained that one of the Habron brothers had shot Police Constable Cock out of spite and revenge. Various witnesses testified to hearing threats made against the police by the brothers and that William had inspected a revolver at an ironmonger's on the afternoon of the shooting. Despite the description given of the man seen at the scene of the shooting by Mr Simpson, elderly and stooping, Constable Beanland was adamant that the man had stood erect and definitely resembled William Habron. Francis Deakin told the court that he was convinced his employees were innocent. He had given the waistcoat to William himself and had probably left the percussion caps in the pockets. On 28 November, after two-and-a-half hours' deliberation, the jury returned a verdict of 'not guilty' against John Habron. William Habron was found 'guilty of wilful murder, with a recommendation for mercy, on the grounds of his youth'.

William was nineteen years old. The judge donned the customary black cap and passed the mandatory sentence of death. For three weeks, William languished in the Condemned Cell, until the Home Secretary, Mr Cross, saw fit to grant a reprieve on 19 December. The sentence was commuted to penal servitude for life and William Habron was sent to Portland Prison as Convict 1547. Throughout the Habron's trial an elderly man with what could accurately be described as a stooping gait, sat in the public gallery of the courtroom watching the proceedings with great interest. At the conclusion of the trial he left Manchester and went to Sheffield. The man's name was Charlie Peace.

Mrs Katherine Dyson. Illustrated Police News

The following evening, Wednesday 29 November, Peace was in the vicinity of Banner Cross Terrace between 7pm and 8pm. He paid a visit to Gregory's shop and asked to speak to the proprietor (John Gregory), but was told he was out. Typically for Charlie in matters where the Dysons were concerned, he proceeded to make a nuisance of himself. Firstly he asked a woman in the street if she would take a message to Kate Dyson for him, asking her to come and see him but the woman refused. Not long before 8pm he approached labourer Charles Brassington, outside the *Banner Cross Hotel*, and began to speak in disparaging terms about the Dysons. Brassington would have nothing to do with Peace and moved away. At 8pm, having put her son to bed, Kate Dyson came downstairs and went to the back parlour where Arthur was sitting in an armchair reading. She sat down for a few moments and about ten minutes later, got up, put on her clogs, left the house by the back door into the moonlit night and went to the privy at the end of the terrace. A short time later, as she opened the door to leave the privy, she was confronted by Charlie Peace, who stood before her with a gun in his hand. Peace called out:

Speak or I'll fire!

Peace confronts Kate Dyson as she is leaving the privy in Banner Cross Terrace. Illustrated Police News

Alarmed, Kate uttered a loud shriek, backed into the privy, slammed the door and locked it. Her husband, on hearing her anguished cry, left the house by the back door and as he emerged round the corner of the building, saw his wife coming out of the privy. He ran towards her, pushing past her as Peace fled down the passage. Dyson followed him then crossed the forecourt and down some steps, whereupon Peace turned and fired a shot at him. It missed but a second shot hit Dyson in the forehead and, as he fell backwards to the ground, his wife, who had followed them exclaimed:

Murder! You villain! You have shot my husband!

Peace fled, hopped over a garden wall and disappeared across a field in the direction of Greystones. In his haste to leave the scene he dropped a packet containing some notes and letters in a field belonging to Mr Else. These items included Dyson's visiting card to him. When examined by police it was observed that the notes were clearly written in a woman's hand and took the form of various requests or assignations. These, Peace later maintained, were Kate's notes and letters to him.

Cole Brothers, Fargate, Sheffield, conducted Arthur Dyson's funeral arrangements. Situated at the junction with High Street and Church Street, the premises of this famous and popular department store was commonly called 'Coles Corner'. Author's collection

Arthur Dyson was carried into the Gregory's house before being transferred to his own house, where Dr Harrison, of Highfield, visited him, and examined him as he was propped up in a chair. The bullet had entered his left temple and lodged in the brain. He died at 10.30pm. Dr Benson arrived shortly afterwards and confirmed Dr Harrison's statement that death had taken place. Police Sergeant Bowler of the Eccleshall Division was in attendance throughout the night, along with constables Crowe and Sylvester. Inspector Bradbury visited the house during the night, then went to make his report at the central police offices.

Mrs Dyson was sufficiently composed in the immediate aftermath following her husband's death to give an interview to a reporter from the *Sheffield and Rotherham Independent*. In what the reporter described as 'with a touch of the Irish brogue' she told him:

Peace is a picture frame dealer by trade. He is a man of very bad character. He used to keep a shop in Scotland street, or

somewhere there, sometime ago. I dare say that would be a year and a half ago. About a years since that he moved to Darnall, and that is the first time we knew anything about him. He is about fifty years of age, about five feet four inches high, with a grey white beard – full beard and moustache. When he came to live by us at Darnall he wanted to make disturbances between me and my husband. He seemed at first to be a very kindly man, having birds and parrots and so on, that he used to talk about. He enticed people to go in and talk. Mr Dyson used to go in, but after a while Peace seemed to put an evil eye upon us, and he then threatened my life. Mr Dyson is out of business. He has been a civil engineer at Tinsley. He is 40 years of age. I have one boy, who is going on five years, and will be five on 11th December. Peace used to come listening at our door. Mr Dyson wrote him a note by postcard demanding him to keep off our premises, as he would have nothing to do with him. The neighbours told us he followed us about wherever we went. He once got up on the Nether Edge bus, and rose with us to Nether Edge, and he did it just to annoy us. One evening I was talking to a neighbour, and he came up. A friend of ours said to him 'It is a shame, listening in that way,' and he [Peace] then came up and presented a revolver at me. That was on the 4th July. I have witnesses to that. He presented the revolver, but did not discharge it. It was a six-barrelled revolver. I then took out a summons against him, but he did not appear. A warrant was then issued, but he was never apprehended. He is a married man, with a wife and family, consisting of a son and daughter. His wife is bottle washer at Messrs. White's liquor store in Church street. His son is employed at Mr Ward's grocer's shop. His daughter is living at home, and I do not think she is employed anywhere. Peace has been before the magistrates before, and they say he was in prison a year or two. We came to live here about six weeks ago. Peace was here the night we moved, and the neighbours tell us now he has been round our doors by day or at night, I don't know which. I went into the yard about a quarter-past-eight o'clock to-night. He was then lying in wait. He had been previously into Mr Gregory's, the grocer, next door. He asked for some tobacco, and went out again. When I was coming out of the closet and was just opening the door, I heard a footstep and thought it was Mr. Gregory. Directly

I had opened the door about a foot, I saw Peace standing there with a revolver in his hand. He said to me, 'Stand and speak, or if you don't I will fire,' or words to that effect. I screamed and shut the door. When I screamed Mr Dyson ran out. He had been reading by the fire, and he ran out in his slippers. I rushed out, and Peace fired, and it missed me when I banged the door. When Mr Dyson ran by he was shot in the front yard. He never spoke after he fell. I rushed to my husband to pick him up to see what was the matter. The neighbours brought him into the house and placed him on a chair. Dr Harrison attended. My husband's brother, Mr Henry Dyson, who lives at 17, Broomfield, also came to see him. Mr Henry Dyson is in the iron business at Messrs. F. Hobson and Co.'s Saville street. My husband fell on his back, with his head towards the road. The shot entered his left temple. Dr Harrison examined him, and saw that the shot had gone right through the brain. It did not come out, but got buried in the brain. Dr. Harrison examined the wound, and told us to look after Mr Dyson, as he was in a very dangerous state. He was unconscious, and died a little before ten o'clock. Peace left Darnall when the warrant was issued, and we do not know where he went to live. I know of no reason but what I have stated why he committed the murder. He tried to make disturbances between me and Mr Dyson, and he did this because he could not succeed. The witnesses have heard him say he would blow my brains out, and my husband's too. He is connected with low, bad places in every city – Manchester, Liverpool, and the other towns. He told Mr Dyson so. Mr Dyson said he was a very bad man, which he knew from some pictures he saw. Peace wrote letters to Mr. Dyson making out he was in Germany to put us off the path. That was when the warrant was taken out, and we knew nothing of him till we moved here six weeks ago. We removed here partly to get rid of him. He told Mr. Gregory he should follow us wherever we went. He did not know Mr Gregory before. He has told people Mr Dyson owed him hundreds of pounds. He is a defamer and a murderer – that is the only name I can call him.

The inquest was opened on Friday 1 December by the coroner, Dossey Wightman, Esquire, at the *Banner Cross Hotel*. On opening the inquiry the coroner said:

I need not explain to you why you are met here. This is a most lamentable case altogether. It appears that a man on whom suspicion rests, the man named Peace, whom in all probability you have all heard of, a man who is suspected at any rate of having caused the death of Mr Arthur Dyson, is not in custody, and the whole affair is so recent that I am exceedingly sorry to say I must adjourn the inquest. I know it is exceedingly grievous to the relations of the deceased, and if I could have seen my way to fulfil my duty and at the same time close the inquiry, I should have been very glad to have done so. But it is clear, it does not admit of a moment's doubt, that the matter is not thoroughly ripe for consideration. I do not know what may turn up, or what more may be known as to the particulars; but at any rate I am in hopes that the man on whom suspicion rests will be found before very long, and produced at the adjourned enquiry. He is entitled to be present if he turns up, and I should like to give him an opportunity of doing so. The question is when will you have it adjourned to. I do not want a long adjournment. I asked Mr Bradbury to see what Mr Jackson [John Jackson the Chief Constable] *has to say.*

Inspector Bradbury said:

About a week or a fortnight; not more, and not much less.

The coroner replied:

That's my idea too. I think it ought to be adjourned for a week.

Inspector Bradbury then handed the coroner documents concerning a letter that had been sent to the Home Secretary regarding the application to offer a reward for the apprehension of a murderer. The Home Secretary had ruled that the application could not be granted until the inquest had been closed. Having perused these documents, Mr Dossey Wightman spoke as follows:

I won't adjourn this for more than a week. I am willing to make it convenient for all parties if I can. Of course Mr Jackson has a duty to perform with regard to this case, so far as the magistrates' court is concerned; and I asked Mr Bradbury to consult him as to how long he thought he should like an adjournment, because of course, if this man has to be apprehended, it is the duty of the police to find him and apprehend him. They seem to think a week will be sufficient. Therefore, I will make it a week, at the same time and place. I suppose some of you come from this neighbourhood, and some from Sheffield? The bulk of them I think from the neighbourhood.

Inspector Bradbury confirmed:

From Brincliffe and Nether Edge.

The coroner then concluded:

I will adjourn the inquest to any house that is convenient to you. What do you say about the Stag Hotel?

This location being generally more convenient to the jury, the coroner bound them over to appear at ten o'clock on the morning of Friday 8 December at the *Stag Hotel*, Sharrow Head. The inquest was then adjourned. Immediately following this, the jury went to Banner Cross Terrace to view the body of Arthur Dyson, which had been laid out at his home there. His widow then formally identified the body and the coroner issued a certificate for burial.

On Monday 4 December the *Sheffield And Rotherham Independent* reported:

The remains of Mr Arthur Dyson, civil engineer, who was murdered by the man Charles Peace, at Banner Cross terrace, Eccleshall road, on Wednesday night, were interred in Eccleshall Churchyard on Saturday afternoon. It was intended that the funeral should be as private as possible, and as the friends of the deceased anticipated that, owing to the very great sensation awakened by the murder, there would be a large attendance of the public, no precise announcement was made as to the hour fixed for the internment…

The funeral was conducted under the auspices of Messrs Cole Brothers of Fargate. The procession left the Dyson's house in Banner Cross Terrace at three o'clock, the weather by that time being raw and damp. Besides the hearse there was just one carriage and that comprised an ordinary cab, there being only four mourners, Mrs Katherine Dyson, her little son and the deceased's brothers, William and Henry Dyson. The plain coffin, made by Mr Elliott of Banner Cross, was almost seven feet in length and adorned with a silver plate bearing the name, age and date of death of the deceased man. Inspector Bradbury escorted the cortege as far as All Saints' Church, where Sergeant Bowler and Police Constable Holgate kept the crowd back at either side of the entrance. The crowd by then was much diminished from that which had gathered in the morning in anticipation of the funeral. After midday when it was believed the funeral would take place, as the weather became even more gloomy than at first light, only those with sufficient fortitude remained. The short procession arrived at the church, where the coffin was met by the vicar, the Rev E Newman at the church gates. The bearers were made up of friends and neighbours of the Dysons, Mr Burnham, Mr R Smithson, Mr J Ogden, Mr G Silcock, Mr J Gregory and Mr J Elliott. Several people were waiting inside the church and some others from the crowd of about a hundred followed the mourners inside the church to attend the service. As the coffin was borne out of the church and taken to the graveside, which was midway between the church and the road leading to the vicarage, the mourners were showered by a steady drizzle of rain. The widow wore a thick veil but even that was not sufficient to disguise her grief from onlookers. It was noticed that her face was bathed in tears as the ceremony drew to a close. Following the internment Mrs Dyson and her son were escorted home by Mr William Dyson. Henry Dyson remained at the church to obtain the vicar's certificate of burial.

The inquest resumed on Friday 8 December at the *Stag Hotel*. A full account leading up to the death of Arthur Dyson and the escape of Charles Peace was heard. Dr J W Harrison provided the medical evidence. He said:

I was fetched about nine o'clock on the night of the murder to see Mr Dyson. I found him sitting in a chair. He was talking, but was insensible. As he was losing blood fast I had him immediately laid on a mattress, and then examined a wound on the left temple. He never recovered consciousness, and died in my presence at about a quarter to eleven o'clock. Mrs Dyson was present and also a man named Gregory. I have since made a post-mortem examination, assisted by Mr John Benson. I found a bruise on the nose and chin, as if the deceased had fallen on his face. The wound on the left temple was about an inch above the external orbit of the eye, and I could pass in the little finger right through it to the skull and into the brain. There was a quantity of effused blood between the skull and the scalp. Upon taking the scalp away from the skull, I found a circular opening in the skull about an inch in diameter. The opening went through the anterior inferior angle of the parietal bone and also through a portion of the spheroid bone. The ball went through the brain in a direction upward and backwards through the left lobe, and was found lodged on the upper surface of that lobe. The bullet was flattened. The fact of it being so flattened is, in my opinion, caused by its coming in contact with the bones already mentioned. The bullet went obliquely and took an upward direction. From this latter fact, I imagine the man who fired the shot was in a lower angle than the deceased. The appearance of the bullet leads me to the conclusion that it was a conical one, but I cannot say it was so positively. I did not make a sufficiently minute examination to say whether the deceased was a healthy man, because the presence of the bullet in the brain fully accounted for death and for all the symptoms I saw ...

In his summing up the coroner said:

I do not intend to call any more evidence, as in all probability the jury will come to a conclusion with that which has been brought before them. As it is, there has been a very full enquiry into the death of the man Arthur Dyson. Inspector Bradbury, I am bound to say, has got up the case exceedingly well, and had anything about the matter and has brought forward apparently every person who knows anything about the matter whose evidence could be of the slightest importance in the inquiry.

Indeed, the only thing he has not done, and that he ought to have, is to have apprehended Peace. I have no doubt, however, that he has tried his best to do so. The jury has first of all to consider how the deceased came by his death, and whether any party, and if so, who, was to blame in the matter. With regard to the cause of death, the jury will no doubt consider the evidence of the medical man, Mr Harrison, quite conclusive. Mr Harrison has made a post-mortem examination, and he has said the cause of death was a bullet to the brain ... You will therefore be satisfied the cause of death was the firing of a bullet from either a gun or a pistol, and that the question is who fired it, and how came the deceased to be shot. The evidence is really very conclusive, and I do not think I need to trouble you with any remarks about it ... You must consider whether you believe the man Charles Peace has been sufficiently identified before yourselves to justify you returning a verdict of wilful murder against him. Of course I need not tell you, as I am sure you know sufficient of the law to understand that if the man Dyson was shot by Peace it was, and must be, wilful murder. Whether malice has been sufficiently proven before you or not does not matter. The law assumed that there was malice if a man killed another wilfully; and consequently the only verdict you should reach would be one of wilful murder. I think the only serious question you have to consider is whether the man was sufficiently identified to justify swearing that it was Peace who shot Mr Dyson ... All you the jury have to do is to satisfy yourselves first, as to whether Mr Dyson was killed by a shot, and if so whether you are satisfied that the man Peace did it. If you are satisfied that is the case then you can only return a verdict of wilful murder against him.

Mr S Langstaff, foreman of the jury, stated that they did not wish to have the evidence read to them, inasmuch as it was very clear. Having retired for a few minutes behind closed doors the jury returned a verdict of wilful murder against Charles Peace. A reward of £100 was offered for his capture. Sometime after the inquest Kate Dyson and her son went to America.

Sheffield Police issued the following description of Peace:

Very slightly built, height 5 feet 4 inches, hair grey; lacking one or more fingers of his left hand; cut marks on the back of both hands; cut marks on forehead; walks with his legs wide apart; speaks somewhat peculiarly, as though his tongue was too large for his mouth, and is a great boaster.

Charlie Peace now used his considerable talent for disguise to its full extent to evade capture. In order to disguise the missing fingers on his left hand, he fashioned a tube which covered his entire arm, to which he added an iron hook. This gave the appearance that his hand and entire arm were missing. He darkened his skin using walnut oil and it was not long before he had established a convincing new identity. He acquired the nickname 'One-armed-Jemmy' and resumed his career as a burglar, travelling from Sheffield to Bristol, Oxford, Derby and Nottingham, before returning to his family in Hull, where his disguise even foxed his daughter, Jenny.

Peace continued to pursue his life of crime. In February 1877, whilst burgling the house of a man named Johnson, he was surprised in the act and, as he fled the scene, fired two shots at Mr Johnson, which fortunately missed the alarmed householder. Not long afterwards he was in Nottingham where he became romantically attached to a young widow. Susan Grey was about thirty years old. She variously called herself by the surnames Bailey and Thompson. Peace was later to describe Susan as being:

… a dreadful woman for drink and snuff…

It was not long before she and Peace were living together as man and wife, calling themselves Mr and Mrs Thompson. He took Susan to Hull, where they took rooms in the house of a police sergeant. As usual Peace resorted to burglary as a means of support. It was not long before the couple moved back to Nottingham, where, one night, police called at the house when Peace and his mistress were in bed. Somehow Peace persuaded the officers to leave the room while he got dressed and he promptly made his escape out of the window. He fled to London and found lodgings in Lambeth. Susan soon joined

Susan Grey, alias Mrs Thompson.
Illustrated Police News

MRS THOMPSON (FROM A PHOTO)

him. He took a shop there at 25 Stangate Street and traded in musical instruments during the day and by night he was augmenting his stock by breaking into houses and filching any instruments that took his eye, as well as other items of value and money. Within weeks of his arrival in Lambeth, Peace moved to Crane Court, in Greenwich and afterwards, in the same district, he took a lease on two adjoining houses there in Billingsgate Street, where he installed himself and Susan in one, and, having persuaded his wife and stepson to move from Hull to join them, installed Hannah and Willie in the other (by this time Peace's daughter, Jenny had married a collier named Bolsover). On 4 May, Peace was in Derby where he robbed an outfitters in London Road, belonging to Mr John Arthur Wailer. Concerning this robbery Peace later commented:

I done a very big mantle place in Derby for a great number of women's mantles and money...

Later, in May, he took a lease on yet another property at 5 East Terrace, Evelina Road, Peckham. He called himself Thompson and claimed to be of independent means. Hannah, who used her previous married name, Ward, lived in the basement with

Charles Peace's house at 5 East Terrace, Evelina Road, Peckham. John D Murray collection

Willie, ostensibly as housekeeper, and Charlie and Susan lived upstairs, where they lived in some style. The rooms were opulently furnished, mostly with items filched by Peace from other people's homes, or paid for with their stolen money. The house was a positive menagerie, being filled with an assortment of dogs, cats, rabbits and a variety of birds including canaries, budgerigars, cockatoos and parrots. Mr Thompson would drive around the district in his pony and trap. He was well dressed and outwardly had all the signs of the respectable self-made man. He looked nothing like the Charles Peace who was wanted for murder in Sheffield. He had dyed his hair black, stained his skin and wore spectacles. Charlie also ventured further around south London in order to select suitable properties to burgle by night. Peace ventured out of London to burgle, visiting such places as Southampton, Portsmouth and Southsea. As time went by the Thompsons became veritable pillars of the local community. They attended church on Sundays and held musical evenings, when Mr Thompson would entertain his guests by playing the fiddle, singing and reciting monologues. Peace spent time working on inventions and attached himself to a man named Brion, to whom he was known as John Ward. One invention, a device for raising sunken vessels, was actually patented. If on the surface all appeared well at 5 Evelina Terrace, to the Thompsons' neighbours, the reality was that tensions ran high within the household. Susan was pregnant and she eventually gave birth to a son. She and Hannah had on more than one occasion argued, and following one particular angry exchange between them, Hannah divulged the details of the Banner Cross murder. Charlie was highly alarmed at this and made both women swear on the bible not to reveal the secret to anyone else and to reconcile their differences.

Life in Peckham continued as usual until Thursday 10 October 1878. Perhaps coincidentally or possibly because, as some believe, someone had tipped the police off, Peace himself maintaining that it was Susan Grey, there was an unusually large police presence patrolling the streets of the south-east London suburb of Blackheath. It was at around 2.00am on the 10 October that Police Constable Edward Robinson noticed a flickering light coming from one room,

Police Constable Robinson struggles with Peace outside 2 St John's Park, Blackheath, on the night of his arrest in October 1878. Illustrated Police News

then another, at the rear of 2 St John's Park, the residence of Mr Burness. Along with Constable William Girling and Sergeant Charles Brown, they went to investigate. While the sergeant went round to the front of the house and rang the doorbell, the two constables secreted themselves by the garden wall at the rear of the house. The moment the doorbell rang the dining room window was opened and a man climbed out. The man was none other than Charlie Peace. As he rushed down the garden path Police Constable Robinson went after him. When the constable was within six yards of Peace, Peace turned round and pointed a revolver at him and called out:

Keep back, keep off, or by God I'll shoot you.

Constable Robinson replied:

You had better not.

Peace fired three shots but all of them missed the constable. As Constable Robinson rushed at Peace another shot was fired, this also missed its target. The constable seized Peace and there was a struggle, during which Peace called out:

You bugger, I'll settle you this time!

A fifth shot rang out and entered the constable's right arm above the elbow. Constable Robinson was determined to get the better of Peace and managed to catch him off balance, flinging him to the ground. He seized the revolver and hit Peace with it several times. As Peace was reaching into a pocket for something as he called out:

You bugger! I'll give you something else!

By this time Constable Girling and Sergeant Brown had arrived at the scene and soon overpowered Peace. As he was being searched Peace attempted to escape but was thwarted by a blow from Constable Girling's truncheon. A few small items of booty were found in his possession, including a spirit flask and cheque book. He also had an array of burglar's tools on his person including a crowbar, jemmy and gimlet. While the wounded policeman was taken to received medical attention, Peace was escorted from Greenwich to Park Row Police Station. There he was charged with the wounding of Police Constable Robinson with intent to murder. He refused to give his name. Inspector John Bonney of Blackheath Road Police Station was put in charge of the case. Later that morning Peace appeared before magistrates at Greenwich, where he still refused to give his name. He was remanded for a week. A letter sent to his co-inventor Mr Brion on 2 November, which Peace signed 'John Ward', in which he expressed concerns that he had not heard from his family, provided the first clue to his identity. Mr Brion, on learning of his associate's activities in Blackheath, set police on the right track. It was, however, Susan Grey who provided the true identity for him and it was she who subsequently applied for, and was given, the £100 reward offered to any person who supplied information leading to the conviction of Peace. Peace's letters of forgiveness to her seem to indicate that this was the case. On discovering that Peace had been arrested Susan and Hannah had removed as much as possible from the house in Peckham. Susan, Hannah and Willie left London and went first to Susan's sister's house in Nottingham. Hannah and her son went on alone to Sheffield, where they decanted to Mr and Mrs Bolsover's house in Hazel Road. The large boxes in Hannah's possession, taken from the house in Peckham were found at Hazel Road on 6 November, after police investigations, following a tip off from Mr Brion, had led them firstly to Susan in Nottingham and shortly afterwards to Hannah. The boxes contained stolen goods that linked John Ward with Charles Peace. Although Hannah was subsequently tried on a charge of receiving stolen goods, she was acquitted, as she was deemed to have acted under the influence of her husband.

Peace was interviewed by Detective Inspector Henry Phillips, the local head of the newly formed Criminal Investigation Department of Scotland Yard. He was taken from Greenwich to Newgate Gaol, where he remained until his trial. When inspectors Bonney and Phillips went to make their report to the Director of the CID, Mr Howard Vincent, the link with Peace and the Banner Cross Murder at Sheffield was established. Detective Inspector Phillips was dispatched to Sheffield to discuss matters with the Chief Constable there.

Charlie Peace was tried under the name of John Ward, alias Charles Peace, at the Central Criminal Court in the Old Bailey on 19 November 1878, before Mr Justice Hawkins, charged with the attempted murder of Police Constable Edward Robinson. Mr Pollard prosecuted and Mr Montague Williams defended. The evidence against him was so substantial it left the jury with no doubt that he was guilty, and having listened to the evidence, came to that conclusion after deliberating for only four minutes. Their verdict was delivered and the clerk of the court, Mr Reed, asked Peace if he had anything to say before judgement was pronounced. Peace then addressed the following remarks to the judge:

My Lord, I have not been fairly dealt with, and I swear before God I never had the intention to kill the policeman. All I meant was to frighten him in order that I might get away. If I had the intention to kill him I could easily have done it. But I never had the intention to kill him. I declare I did not fire five shots. I only fired four shots … If your Lordship will look at the pistol you will see that it goes off very easily, and the sixth barrel went off of its own accord after I was taken into custody at the station. At the time the fifth shot was fired the constable had hold of my arm and the pistol went off quite by accident. I really did not know the pistol was loaded, and I hope, my Lord, you will have mercy upon me. I feel I have disgraced myself and am not fit to live or die. I am not prepared to meet my God, but I feel that my career has been made to appear much worse than it really is. Oh my Lord, do have mercy upon me, and I assure you that you shall never repent it. Give me one more chance of repenting and preparing myself to meet my God. As you hope for mercy yourself at the hands of the great God, do have mercy upon me, a most wretched miserable man – a man that am not fit to die. I am not fit to live, but with the help of my God, I will try to become a good man.

Apparently unmoved by the remarks just made to him by the prisoner in the dock, Mr Justice Hawkins sentenced him to penal servitude for life. The judge recommended Constable Robinson for promotion and for a reward of £25. Constable Robinson was duly promoted to sergeant. Following his trial Peace was taken to Pentonville Prison. Matters were already in hand to indict him for the Banner Cross Murder.

On Friday 17 January 1879, Peace was taken from Pentonville Prison, where he was serving his sentence, and conveyed to Sheffield by train to appear at Sheffield Town Hall before Mr Welby, the stipendiary magistrate for a committal hearing. Mrs Katherine Dyson, who had returned from the United State of America to give evidence, was the first witness. It was decided that her cross-examination would take place at the next hearing and the proceedings were adjourned. Peace was taken back to London.

Early on the morning Wednesday 22 January Peace was removed from Pentonville, in handcuffs, and accompanied by two warders to catch the 5.15am express to Sheffield for the second hearing. The train was due to arrive at 8.15am. Peace had on his previous journey to Sheffield kept making excuses to leave the carriage whenever the train stopped, to relieve himself. In anticipation of this occurring again the warders had provided themselves with small waterproof bags, which Peace could use when the need took him and these could then be disposed of out of the carriage window. Shortly after the train had passed through Worksop, Peace asked for one of the bags. The 6-inch chain on the handcuffs Peace was wearing enabled him sufficient movement to attend to his own needs. He faced the window and duly emptied his bladder. As the window was being lowered in order to dispose of the bag, Peace leaped out of it. Whilst one of the warders sprang towards him and caught him by the left foot, Peace, grasped hold of the carriage's footboard and proceeded to kick at the warder with his right foot. There was insufficient space for the other warder to come to the aid of his colleague and the struggle continued as the train thundered on for another two miles, all the time the other warder desperately trying to pull the communication cord to stop the train, which for some

Peace attempts to make his escape on the train journey to Sheffield. Illustrated Police News

reason would not activate. Peace eventually managed to kick off his left shoe, whereupon he fell to the ground as the train travelled on. With the assistance of passengers in other carriages the warders succeeded in pulling up the train. As the train continued on its journey the warders ran back along the line. Peace was found lying by the side of the track unconscious on the snow-covered ground. He was bleeding from a head wound. He regained consciousness shortly and was soon complaining that he was in great pain and dying from cold. He was taken back to Sheffield in the guard's van of a slow train heading in that direction, where they arrived at 9.20am. News had already reached Sheffield Police Court that Peace had absconded from the train. The crowded courtroom heard the Chief Constable tell the bench that Peace had escaped. The court carried on with its normal business and sometime later heard that Peace was once again in custody but he had been injured and his attendance in court that day was unlikely. Peace received medical attention in one of the police cells from the Police Surgeon, Dr Stewart and Mr Arthur Hallam, a surgeon from Sheffield. He had a severe scalp wound and was suffering from concussion of the brain. He was eventually pronounced sufficiently fit to appear before the magistrate on 30 January.

The public were showing considerable interest in the case and to avoid the possibility of any scenes in the courtroom the hearing was held in a dingy corridor outside Peace's cell in the Town Hall. Peace was seated in an armchair and grumbled often about the cold. He was represented by the Sheffield solicitor, William E Clegg. Mr Clegg's other claim to fame was having played football for both Sheffield Wednesday and England. In his cross-examination of Mrs Dyson Mr Clegg set out to show that her relationship with Peace was of a far more intimate nature than she had been prepared to reveal and that Arthur Dyson had been killed in the course of a struggle in which he had been the aggressor. Mrs Dyson's inability to remember certain facts and the letters dropped by Peace in Mr Else's field as he fled from Banner Cross Terrace, some of which were read to the Court, seemed to add credence to Mr Clegg's assertions. However, Mrs Dyson remained adamant in her denial that any struggle had taken place between Peace and her husband. The proceedings ended with Peace being

The escape and recapture of Peace. Illustrated Police News

committed to take his trial at Leeds Assizes. As Peace was escorted to the railway station to catch the train that would take him to Wakefield Prison, a large crowd had gathered to witness his departure. He appeared old and feeble and was wearing his convict suit, with its cap perched on top of the white bandage that bound his head and contrasted sharply with his brown complexion. He remained in Wakefield until the eve of his trial when he was taken to Armley Gaol in Leeds.

Charles Peace was tried at Leeds Assizes on Tuesday 4 February before Mr Justice Lopes (afterwards Lord Ludlow). The trial lasted one day. Mr Campbell Foster, QC, led for the prosecution and Peace was represented by Mr Frank Lockwood and Mr Stuart Wortley.

In his opening remarks Mr Campbell Foster contended that the shooting of Arthur Dyson by Charles Peace was premeditated and committed with 'malice of afterthought'. During Katherine Dyson's evidence, which was vociferously challenged by Peace's defence, Peace leant forward in his armchair which was set within a semi-circular spiked enclosure, looking at her fixedly and occasionally summoning his solicitor and whispering to him. There were various witnesses who corroborated the events on the night of the shooting. Evidence was given concerning Peace's threats to the

Charles Peace sitting in the dock at his trial at Leeds Assizes on 4 February 1879, drawn by his defence counsel, Frank Lockwood. Illustrated Police News

Dysons in July 1876. Then evidence concerning his arrest in Blackheath in October 1878, during which the revolver he had used was produced. There was tentative evidence that the rifling corresponded with the bullet extracted from the skull of Arthur Dyson and with the bullets fired on the night of Peace's arrest in Blackheath. In defence, Mr Lockwood addressed the jury in an attempt to persuade them that the death of Arthur Dyson was the accidental result of a struggle between Peace and himself.

In his summing up Mr Justice Lopes invited the jury to take the revolver in their hands, try the trigger and to see for themselves whether they believed the gun could go off accidentally. He said that Mr Lockwood had been perfectly justified in his attempts to discredit Mrs Dyson's evidence but that the case did not rest on her evidence alone. In his opinion it had been clearly proved that no struggle or scuffle had taken place before the murder. He urged the jury not to lay themselves open to the reproach that they had wrongfully taken away the life of a fellow man. He added that the plea of provocation failed altogether where preconceived ill-will against the deceased was proved. He concluded by saying that if the defence rested on no solid foundation, then the jury must do their duty to the community at large and by the oath they had sworn.

The jury retired at 7.15pm and ten minutes later returned with their verdict. They found the prisoner guilty. When the Clerk of Arraigns asked Peace if he had anything to say, he replied in a barely audible voice:

It is no use my saying anything.

Mr Justice Lopes then donned the black cap and passed the following sentence of death:

Charles Peace, after a most patient trial and after every argument has been urged by your learned counsel which ingenuity could suggest, you have been found guilty of the murder of Arthur Dyson by a jury of your country. It is not my duty, still my desire, to aggravate your feelings at this moment by a recapitulation of any portion of the details of what, I fear, I can only call your criminal career. I implore you during the short time that may remain to you to live to prepare for eternity. I pass upon you the only sentence which the law permits in a case of this kind. That sentence is that you be taken from this place to the place whence you came and thence to a place of execution and that you be there hanged by the neck until you are dead…

Peace remained composed as he was taken from the court and back to Armley Gaol. It would appear that he took notice of Mr Justice Lopes' words to him regarding his preparation for eternity. He became thoroughly penitent. During his incarceration Peace was visited by the Reverend J H Littlewood, Vicar of Darnall, to whom he confessed all his crimes, including the revelation that four months before he had killed Arthur Dyson; and had shot Police Constable Cock at Whalley Range. He said that he had intended to break into the house but was spotted by two policemen. As he tried to make his escape he ran into Cock's arms. Peace said he fired his gun wide to frighten the constable but when he continued to come at him, he aimed straight and shot him in the chest. Peace said:

I got away, which was all I wanted. Some time later I saw in the papers that certain men had been taken into custody for the murder of this policeman. That interested me. I thought I should like to attend the trial, and I determined to be present. I left Hull for Manchester, not telling my family where I had gone. I attended the Manchester Assizes for two days, and heard the youngest of the brothers, as I was told they were, sentenced to death. The sentence was afterwards reduced to penal servitude for life. Now, sir, some people will say I was a hardened wretch for allowing an innocent man to suffer for my crime. But what man would have done otherwise in my position? Could I have done otherwise, knowing, as I did, that I should certainly be hanged for the crime? But now that I am going to forfeit my own life, and feel that I have nothing to gain by further secrecy, I think it right, in the sight of God and man, to clear this young man, who is innocent of the crime.

Peace writes his will at Armley Gaol.
Illustrated Police News

Charles Peace in the condemned cell at Armley Gaol. Illustrated Police News

Police needed to be convinced that Peace was telling the truth and not pulling a fast one by trying to get a convict free under false pretences. They interviewed him concerning the sequence of events on the night of the murder and drew a map of the area. He was able to describe his movements in such detail and pinpoint on the map exactly where and what had occurred that left no doubt he was telling the truth. Following Charlie Peace's revelations William Habron was given a free pardon and compensation of £800.

Peace spent a great deal of time writing letters. He had forgiven Susan for betraying him and, although he desperately wanted to see her, had acceded to his family's wishes that he should not. On Monday 24 February 1879, the day before his execution, Peace was visited in the condemned cell by Hannah, Willie and his daughter; and her husband. He was in good spirits. Before they departed, at his wife's request, Peace knelt and prayed with them all. As Hannah was leaving the cell, Peace handed her a card which he asked should be printed as his funeral card. It read:

> *In Memory of Charles Peace*
> *who was executed at Armley Prison,*
> *Tuesday, February 25th 1879.*
> *For that I don* [sic] *but never intended.*

The following morning it was bitterly cold. Charles Peace rose at 6am and spent some time writing letters. He ate a hearty breakfast, although he saw fit to complain about the quality of the bacon. Afterwards a warder rebuked him for the amount of time he was spending in the lavatory and banged on the door. On hearing this Peace called out:

> *You are in a hell of a hurry. Are you going to be hanged or am I?*

When William Marwood, the executioner arrived, Peace remained calm. This is Marwood's own account of what followed:

> *...A firmer step never walked to the scaffold... I admired his bravery; he met his fate like a man; he acknowledged his guilt, and*

William Marwood, who executed Peace. Author's collection

his faith in God with regard to his future was very good ... During the seven years I have officiated as executioner I never met a man who faced death with greater calmness. It's true he shivered a bit; but not through fear. It was a bitter winter's morning, and he complained of the cold ... The bravery was an outcome of his nature. He was ignorant alike of weakness and timidity ... He had been suffering with a bad cough for some days. The night before his execution he said to one of his warders, 'I wonder whether Mr Marwood can cure this bad cough of mine?' To which the warder replied, 'I have no doubt he could.' And I can tell you that a man who jokes about getting hanged to cure a cough is no coward ... He died instantly. But perhaps I had better tell you what occurred just before the execution: it is a most curious thing. He had got hold of the idea that I should terribly punish him at the scaffold and he repeatedly asked the chief warder to be sure to tell me that he wished for an interview about a quarter of an hour before he was led out to die. Accordingly, ten minutes to eight o'clock I went to the condemned cell, which stands about in the centre of the gaol, some hundred yards from the place where the scaffold was erected. Peace was seated, he was in his convict dress, and there were several officials attending upon him. The bandage had been removed from his head [Peace's head had been bandaged in consequence of the injury he received on the train journey taking him to be tried in Sheffield]*; and he did not wear spectacles. He was neither weak nor prostate, but sat upright in his chair, as if he had never known a moment's illness. When I appeared in the doorway, he seemed pleased, and holding out his hand said, 'I am glad to see you Mr Marwood. I wish to have a word with you. I do hope you will not punish me. I hope you will do your work quickly'. 'You will not suffer pain from my hand' I replied;and then Peace, grasping my arm, said, 'God bless you. I hope to meet you all in Heaven. I am thankful to say my sins are all forgiven'. It was now time to pinion him. He stood up at my request, but did not really need the support of the two warders by his side. He was not at all nervous, and quietly submitted to my operations. Pinioning is a very ingenious process. I run a main strap round the body, and connected to it are two other straps, which take the small of the arm, so that the elbows are fastened close to the body and the hands are free. Peace complained, saying, 'The straps fit very tight.' I replied, 'It is better so; it will prevent you from suffering.' He made no further objection, and taking hold of the main strap, so as to keep my hand on him, we started for the scaffold. The Governor and the Under-Sheriff went first, then came the Chaplain; and I followed with the condemned man, two warders attending him, one on each side. They grasped him by the arms, but did not support him. He was bareheaded. His face was pale, but pinched with cold rather than fear. As he arrived near the scaffold he gave a very wistful look at my arrangements. They were all right, and seemed to satisfy him, for he made no remark. He went up the step leading to the drop with a firm tread, whilst the Chaplain read the burial service. I brought him to a proper stand under the crossbar, and then strapped his legs. When that was done he wished to say something to the reporters, and made a beautiful speech. Such a speech has never come from a condemned man I have executed. It was a really good speech. When he had finished it he asked for a drink; but you know that was unreasonable, and it could not be admitted, for the time fixed for the execution had fully expired. So I placed the cap over his face, and adjusted the rope, when he said: 'I say, the rope fits very tight!' I replied: 'Never mind; its all for the best; hold up your chin', and he did so immediately, so that I could* *properly fix the rope. 'Goodbye all; God bless you,' he kept repeating as I went towards the lever. At this time he did not require anyone to support him, but I told one of the warders to take hold of the back strap. Whilst he stood in this manner on the drop with the noose round his neck, I pushed the lever forward; it withdrew the bolt from the swinging doors, and Peace's body fell through the aperture beneath the platform. The drop was exactly nine feet four inches. Peace was dead in a moment; he never moved a finger or a muscle after he fell; so I carried out my promise to do it well and quickly.*

Following his execution, after Charles Peace's body had been allowed to hang for the customary one hour, it was taken down and laid out. Afterwards the body was viewed by the jury at the inquest held later that day. Charles Peace was then buried within the precincts of Armley Gaol. For some time after Peace's execution the waxwork effigy of him that became a popular exhibit at Madame Tussaud's was accompanied by a waxwork of Police Constable Edward Robinson.

Charles Peace was buried within the precincts of Armley Gaol. Peace's body having been placed in a coffin is being covered with lime by a warder prior to burial. Illustrated Police News

CHAPTER 4

The Shelf Street Hatchet Murder

1881

… looking through the kitchen window she saw her father come from the front room into the kitchen. He was carrying a hatchet, which was dripping with blood.

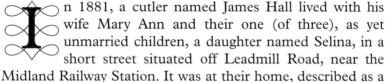n 1881, a cutler named James Hall lived with his wife Mary Ann and their one (of three), as yet unmarried children, a daughter named Selina, in a short street situated off Leadmill Road, near the Midland Railway Station. It was at their home, described as a cottage in contemporary accounts, at 149 Shelf Street, that one of the most horrific murders to take place in Sheffield in living memory occurred on the night of Saturday 26 March.

The Halls' home was situated at the corner of Shelf Street and Leadmill Road and was a very humble affair consisting of only a kitchen, living room and one bedroom. The entrance was in Shelf Street and nailed on the back of the door was a horseshoe, 'for luck'. 'Good fortune keeps the house the horse-shoe's in', so the proverb goes. The window that lit the small kitchen faced onto the back yard, the two other windows of the dwelling in the downstairs living room and the upstairs bedroom faced on to Leadmill Street. James Hall, aged fifty-three, a spring-knife cutler, was employed at Messrs Thomas Turner and Co's Suffolk Works.

At one time Hall was industrious but more recently he had become somewhat work shy, and some called him an idle, dissolute fellow, to whom loafing apparently came naturally. He could rarely be bothered to go to work. Several of his neighbours didn't have a great deal to say in his favour. According to them his chief occupation was begging in the street and playing dominoes in public houses. He belonged to a fraternity of like-minded loafers who habitually stood at street corners with a halfpenny in their open hand begging for another to add to it with which to buy bread. By this method the 'beggar' usually had collected enough to keep him in beer for the night and the custom was always to keep a halfpenny with which to resume 'business' the following morning. His twenty-four-year-old daughter, Selina, was later to say that in the fortnight leading up to her mother's death her father hadn't worked at all and the most he had brought home during recent years was 10*s*. last 'bull week'. The neighbours, however, if they had little to say in James Hall's favour, a man they generally regarded as behaving like a vagabond, they had nothing but good to say about his wife. She was a pleasant, hard-working woman who, despite her husband's shortcomings, made every effort to keep the family home together by taking in washing and doing other domestic duties around the town.

It seems that Hall was unable to appreciate his wife's self-sacrifice and industry. In fact far from being appreciative he became resentful and as his drinking increased so did his moody fits. He had, on more than one occasion, threatened to murder not only his wife but also his daughter. This morbid desire seemed to seldom be far from his thoughts and a few weeks before the murder took place Hall had once again threatened to murder his wife; and tauntingly had a hatchet sharpened for the purpose, soon after his daughter had taken the edge off it chopping up fish.

On Saturday 26 March, Hall passed the earlier part of the day drinking and returned home in a semi-intoxicated state at four o'clock. Mrs Hall was out working, charing for a Mr Sewell, in Broomhill, but Selina was at home. Her father was quick to ask what had been prepared for him for tea and expressed his preference for beefsteak or at the very least sausages. Selina told him he could have neither and as he had brought no money into the house he would have to make do with tea and dry bread or toast. He became very angry and further demanded that he should be given beefsteak or sausages, then stormed out of the house and didn't return until well after eight o'clock. Selina was still at home and when Hall asked where her mother was she told him she had gone to the shop to make some purchases and would soon be back. Mrs Hall returned and some angry words were exchanged. At nine o'clock, Selina left the house with her mother, as Hall protested that his wife should not go out. Mrs Hall ignored her husband and went to visit her married daughter in Howard Street and then her son in Leadmill Road. Selina left the house to go out with her fiancée, Richard Duckenfield, a scissor grinder, who lived at 28 New George Street and she met him in the town and they went together to the *White Hart Inn*, in Waingate.

At eleven o'clock a neighbour, Mr Benjamin Betts, was passing the Halls' house when he saw Mrs Hall leaning against the doorpost. As she rested her head upon her hand, she said to him:

My husband has been striking me with a hatchet.

Believing Mrs Hall to be exaggerating the situation, as he saw no blood on her, and that the quarrel was not of a serious nature, Mr Betts replied:

James Hall confronts his daughter, Selina, having murdered his wife, Mary Ann, with a hatchet. Illustrated Police News

Oh, nonsense; go in and agree.

Mrs Hall was not seen alive again, except by her murderer.

At 11.20pm, Selina Hall returned to Shelf Street with her fiancée and found the door was locked. As Selina said goodnight to Dick, as she referred to him, she went to the back yard to get the key from a hook secreted near the kitchen window, where it was common practice to leave it when the family were out. On looking through the kitchen window she saw her father come from the front room into the kitchen. He was carrying a hatchet, which was dripping with blood. She immediately feared that he had done her mother some injury and let out a loud scream, which her father heard and rushed to open the door, possibly with the intention of making his escape. As Selina began to speak to her father, he aimed a blow at her with the hatchet, which with considerable presence of mind, she managed to deflect with her umbrella, the blade striking her on the chin, and fortunately giving her only a slight cut. She screamed 'Murder!' and her fiancée came back within seconds, having heard her first scream and immediately

The Halls' home in Shelf Street, which stood at the corner of Leadmill, with its door in Shelf Street and its living room and bedroom windows facing on to Leadmill Road. James Hall is seen pursuing his daughter, Selina, with a hatchet, with which he attempts to strike her. Selina fends the blow off with her umbrella, while her finacee, Richard Duckenfield comes to her assistance. Illustrated Police News

sprang to her aid. He got her to safety, and at considerable personal risk, seized Hall as he attempted to strike him with a blow from the hatchet, wrestled with him, and succeeded in tripping him up and disarming him as he crashed to the ground when the hatchet was forced from his hand. With the help of three other young men – Henry Mosley and Henry Merrill, of Matilda Street, and William Wentworth, of Fornham Street – who had heard the commotion and quickly arrived at the scene, they were able to prevent Hall escaping and kept him out in the street until the police arrived. Police Constable William Crowe was on duty in St Mary's Road, on hearing the cry 'Murder!' he hurried in the direction of Leadmill Road, where the cry appeared to have come from. On his way there he was met by a youth, who told him that a man had murdered his wife in Shelf Street. Upon turning into Leadmill Road, he saw Hall on the ground with Duckenfield and some other men holding him down.

The policeman entered the house and, on going into the living room, a gruesome sight confronted him. The fireplace was in the centre of the wall facing the door with a recess at each side. In the recess between the fireplace and the window lay the body of Mary Ann Hall. She was laying almost at full length with her face uppermost and her head slightly twisted towards the wall. The head had practically been cleft in two, the whole of the right side caved in and brain tissue was protruding from her wounds. Her upper body was a mass of gore and the paintwork, wallpaper and furniture was bespattered with blood. On satisfying himself that the woman was dead, Constable Crowe left the house and returned to Leadmill Road, where Hall was still in the clutches of Duckenfield and the other men.

Hall was taken to Highfields Police Station in London Road. He seemed unconcerned when he was arrested and during his removal to the police station he said very little. He was clearly under the influence of alcohol and during the journey said: 'I hope I have done the ——.' On arrival at the police station, he was asked his name in Inspector Bradbury's presence, he did not hesitate to give it, and added: 'I did it myself, and intended to do it.' The hatchet, which was smeared with blood, was also taken to the police station. When Hall was searched he was found to have a purse containing 10s. 10½d. in his possession. Inspector Bradbury then went to Shelf Street with Constable Crowe and some other officers. The police surgeon for the division, Mr William Dale James, was sent for and he arrived from his London Road residence and pronounced Mary Ann Hall dead.

James Hall was subsequently removed to the Central Police Offices, to await his appearance before the stipendiary magistrate on Monday morning. On Monday 29 March, James Hall appeared before Mr Edward Welby, at Sheffield Town Hall. The Chief Constable, Mr Jackson said:

> *The prisoner is charged with the wilful murder of his wife. It will be necessary to have a post-mortem examination of her today. I shall be able to call one witness now, then ask your worship to be good enough to grant a demand. The inquest on the body of the woman has not yet been fixed.*

Richard Duckenfield was then called. During the course of his evidence the Chief Constable asked him:

> *When you heard her scream 'Murder!' did you go back?*

Duckenfield replied: *Yes; and then I saw the prisoner running after her with something in his hand, but I did not see what it was.*

Jackson continued: *Did you see him do anything to the daughter?*

Duckenfield said: *No; he ran after her but could not catch her, and when I had got nearly close to him he turned round and struck at me with a hatchet similar to the one produced. He did not hit me. I then ran away, and he followed me down the street. The daughter also came running after us, and she called out to me, 'Dick, he has a hatchet in his hand.' When she got nearly close to the prisoner, he turned round and was just going to hit her with the hatchet, when I got hold of his arm and threw him on his back ... When I got him on his back I struck him several times. The hatchet then had fallen out of his hand ...*

At the conclusion of Mr Duckenfield's evidence the Chief Constable asked for the prisoner to be remanded, and Hall was duly remanded for a week.

The inquest was held the following morning, Tuesday 29 March, at the *Royal Standard Hotel*, St Mary's Road, before the coroner, Dossey Wightman, Esquire. The foreman of the jury was Mr William Monnsey. The prisoner was brought to the hotel in a cab, accompanied by Detective Wormack. A large crowd had gathered outside the hotel in anticipation of his arrival. As Hall was taken out of the cab and into the hotel he was hooted and booed. Selina Hall was the first witness to be called. After saying that her mother was a healthy woman and

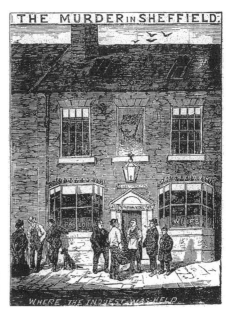

The Royal Standard Hotel, *St Mary's Road, where the inquest was held.* Illustrated Police News

that she had never had a doctor's bill in her life. She spoke about the events of the previous Saturday, and after saying that afternoon her mother was engaged in charing added:

I was employed at Mr. Ibottson's, edge tool maker, until half-past two in the afternoon. I left home at half-past eight in the morning. My mother was then in the house, getting her breakfast. I did not see my father that morning: he went out about half-past seven. When I returned home at half-past two, I found my mother…I went out again into the next neighbour's house to polish a machine top, and I did not return to my parent's home until half-past four the same afternoon. I did not find anyone was in then, and I remained at home.

Miss Hall then described her father's return and him asking for beefsteak or sausages. She then went on to describe how he had left again in a temper. Under further questioning she was prompted to say:

… When he came in I was upstairs and he called to me. I suppose he thought mother was upstairs, because he shouted, 'Polly, I'm not going out tonight.' My mother was called Mary Ann, but he always called her Polly…

Richard Duckenfield was the next witness called and he gave an account of his relationship with Selina Hall, which had spanned some seven years, as well as the events leading up to James Hall's arrest. The men who had helped him hold Hall until the police arrived were called next and then Mr William Dale James, Police Surgeon. Mr Dale James said:

I am a police surgeon and I never attended this woman during life. I did not know her. I have made a post-mortem examination, and I find there are seven wounds, six on the head and one on the throat, going from right to left. There is one on the right side of the head which has cut through the scalp two inches long, and cut a piece out of the skull.

The coroner: *Would that be a wound made by a blunt, dull instrument, or by a sharp one?*

Mr James: *It must have been a sharp instrument. The wound next to that is three inches long, and passes through scalp and skull into the brain. It had also been done by a sharp instrument. The next wound is at the back of the crown of the head, and is one three-quarters of an inch long, and passes through scalp and skull into the brain. The next forms nearly the whole left hand side of the head. Nearly the whole of the left side of the head is destroyed.*

The coroner: *Cut literally to pieces?*

Mr James: *The whole of the left side of the head from the ear is cut away, probably the result of many blows.*

The coroner: *Exposing the brain, or cutting part of it off?*

Mr James: *Crushing it out, sir; destroying it.*

The coroner: *That is probably the result of many blows?*

Mr James: *Yes. Then there is another wound below that cutting the ear in two, and cutting the top of the jaw bone and the bone at the back – the temporal. That is the left ear. There is another wound immediately below this, cutting through the skin and muscles of the neck, and has wounded the angle of the jaw.*

The coroner: *Now in your opinion have all these wounds been done by a sharp instrument?*

Mr James: *Yes. There is another triangular shallow wound on the left side of the neck. That hatchet* [produced and shown to the jury] *would produce the wounds. The body was otherwise healthy. The cause of death is the injuries to the head which I have described.*

The coroner: *Death was almost instantaneous.*

Mr James: *Yes.*

The coroner: *You don't see anything at all improbable, supposing it is given in evidence that this woman had been seen a few minutes before the injuries, she might have received those injuries, and then been dead a few minutes after being alive and well?*

Mr James: *Certainly.*

The prisoner: *You say she had a stroke upon the head before eleven?*

The coroner: *How can the surgeon tell you that? He cannot possibly tell it. He knows nothing about it at all except what he found at the post-mortem.*

Prisoner: *He said instantaneous a bit since.*

The coroner: *He said the wounds he saw were sufficient to cause death, but instantaneous is a very strong expression.* [Addressing the witness Mr William Dale James] *Can you say within what time of receiving these wounds the woman would die?*

Mr James: *By the time she had received all these wounds she would be dead.*

The coroner: *In about what time would she receive them all?*

Mr James: *There were seven blows at least, and with the destruction of the left side of the head, she would not survive that.*

The coroner: *Then that is instantaneous?*

Mr James: *It is.*

The coroner: *You don't think it probable that she might walk out again after the first blow?*

Mr James: *She might have the first blow -*

The coroner: *But you don't know where the first blow was?*

Mr James: *If the first blow I have described was the first in point of time, she might have been able to walk out to the door, but she would not be able to walk after receiving all the blows. There would be no living after that.*

The coroner: *You know nothing about the first or second blows. You know there are those marks on her head and that they have produced death. Mr Hall [the prisoner] wants to ask about a previous blow given in evidence by a previous witness. This witness [Mr William Dale James] does not know anything about that, Hall.*

Mr James: *There were some bruises upon the arms.*

The coroner: *When you get a person with such injuries as these, I can never get rid of the idea that it is no good going in for these small bruises and contusions. Supposing there are contusions on the arms, it seems to me, if they were inflicted anytime before the 25th, they did not matter, because they would not kill the woman, and if inflicted on the 25th, they are so trivial as compared with the greater injuries which cause her death as to be unimportant.*

Prisoner: *If I had never seen her about eleven o'clock, and somebody else had done all this here-*

The coroner: *That is your look out. If you can prove that, you will be a very lucky man but it will rest with you to prove it.*

Constable Crowe then gave his evidence, saying:

> *...I went into the house and there I saw the woman lying on her back on the floor, and she appeared to be dead. I then came out and got hold of Hall, and Wentworth assisted me in getting him up off the ground. I then took him into custody and conveyed him to the Highfield Police-station, straight off. I did not go into the house again...I returned to the house...I saw the deceased...in the same position in which she was when I was there before...Inspector Baradbury was in the house and he sent me to fetch Dr James...he pronounced her dead in my presence. That would be about half-past two o'clock on the Sunday morning...*

Inspector Bradbury: *...I came down to the house. I saw blood and brains splashed upon the wall five or six feet high.*

The coroner: *Five or six feet high?*

Inspector Bradbury: *Yes sir, some of it was on the pictures and I should think, and I should think they would be about six feet high up at least. I took her upstairs and laid her on the mattress, and sent for the doctor, I then returned to Highfield Police Station.*

Further evidence was given concerning Hall's condition at the police station regarding his state of intoxication. That concluded the police evidence. The coroner then addresses Hall, saying:

> *You are entitled to give evidence or to make a statement if you like, but it is my duty to tell you that whatever you do say will be taken down in writing and may be used against you on your trial.*

Prisoner: *Then I have nothing to say.*

The coroner: *You are not bound to say anything unless you like.*

Prisoner: *Then I'll save it to another day.*

In his summing up the coroner told the jury:

> *... your duty in this matter is to ascertain, as at every inquest, the cause of death of the deceased person ; and secondly, whether any person or persons was or were to blame for the death ... it would be impossible for men in their senses to believe that a man could inflict such wounds on another person without intending them to lead to the death of that person. The evidence is so exceedingly clear that there really seems no point on which to direct you.*

The jury left the room and returned after deliberating for ten minutes with a verdict of 'guilty of wilful murder'. The coroner then addressed the prisoner as follows:

> *The jury have returned a verdict of wilful murder against you, in this case, and it is my duty to commit you for trial for wilful murder. You will be taken from here to the Town Hall, and in all probability brought before the magistrate, after which you will have to go to Wakefield to await your trial at the next assizes for murder. It is a case in which you cannot have bail granted you, and, therefore it is not worth your while trying the matter at all. You will be kept in custody on this commitment until your trial.*

The proceedings lasted three hours. As Hall was brought out of the *Royal Standard Hotel* handcuffed to Detective-Officer Wormack, a crowd of about 300 had gathered outside. As he was hurriedly taken to the cab, he was spat at by the women and jeered, booed and cursed for being a coward by the men. The coroner having made out a warrant committing him to trial, Hall was later taken to Wakefield Gaol.

Hall was brought back to Sheffield on 30 March, for another appearance before the stipendiary magistrate. At the end of the case for the prosecution Hall was formally charged with murder. When Mr Welby asked the prisoner if he had anything to say, Hall replied:

It will not take me many minutes to say what I have to say ... It is stated by one witness that I have threatened my wife many a time in my life. That is true.

Mr Welby: *Do you wish this writing down?*

Prisoner: *Yes, it's true, I say. The reason was this. Three year sin' I lived on Paternoster Row. It war a double house, front door and back kitchen door. There wur a yard behind and a passage coming into the street the back way to make an entrance there. I went home one night. There wur no one in the house and the middle kitchen door wur closed. Well, I thewt where wur my wife. I tried to open t' door an' I couldn't exactly get it open, as there were summat behind. I pushed hard and as I go in't back kitchen door opened. My wife thrust me back into t' house through t' middle door. I thowt there were summat wrong so I went forward to t' back kitchen window and I see a man going down t' passage on his tip toes. Thinks I 'That's William Lowe,' and I runs to t' bottom of t'passage and saw it wur him getting over t'wall into t' front street. So I goes back and says 'Who were yon man in t'house wi' thee?' She says 'What man?' I says 'The man that's just gone out of t' kitchen door when I came in. She says 'There was no man with me.' I says 'I see him going down the passage and leap over t' wall out of t' way. She says 'Who wur it? I says I know t' man. I says 'I know his first name but not his second exactly.' She says 'It's queer you should know his first name and not his second.' I says 'Why, because there's two half brothers, both by one mother, but two fathers an' I says 'I don't know which name its is, whether its Lowe or Booth.' 'Well,' she says 'there's been no one wi me.' I says 'If I ever catch thee at owt of sort I'll have thee life'. That's all about that. I've seen bits of things many a time after. I says 'Don't let me catch thee else I shall do*

> *as I said.' Well, I went home last Saturday night.*
> *Well, I saw her about a quarter past eleven and goes*
> *through t' kitchen into t' house. There wur a man*
> *and her on t' sofa. I says 'What sort of game's this*
> *Poll?' I asked flying towards t' man to get hold of*
> *him. He kicks t' round table against me and flies*
> *out of t' door. I picks t' table up, runs to t' door but*
> *he has gone. I comes back and I says 'Now what*
> *dost think about thyself?' She says 'Now thou hast*
> *done as thou like, I shall do as I like.' I said 'Wilt*
> *thou?' 'Ay lad' she says. So wi me having a drop of*
> *beer I goes unto t' cupboard and gets t' hatchet and*
> *I says 'I'll do as I like' Then I struck her. She fell*
> *on t' ground. I struck her again and again. Thinks*
> *I 'Well she's dead.' Then my daughter came. The*
> *door was not locked. It sticks at times. I told her it*
> *was not locked. She called me a liar. I was agitated*
> *and I struck her.*

Having finished speaking, the transcribed statement he had just given was read over to him. Hall, on being satisfied that what had been taken down was absolutely correct, signed the statement with a cross.

The funeral of the murdered woman took place on Wednesday 30 March, during the afternoon. A large crowd had gathered in Leadmill Road and Edmund Road in anticipation of the cortege passing by. Outside the cottage in Shelf Street where the murder took place and where the dead woman's coffin was resting, police found it difficult to keep the crowd from pushing forward, as it was estimated to number 3,000. As the coffin was brought out of the house and placed in the hearse, a sudden surge by those nearest the front strained police resources. They struggled to prevent some of the crowd pushing rudely against the relatives of the dead woman, as they were boarding the two omnibuses which had been provided for the mourners.

Into the first of the omnibuses the murdered woman's daughter, Miss Selina Hall, had to be almost carried, such was her grief. Miss Hall was supported by her suitor, Mr Richard

Duckenfield, and her brother, Mr Abraham Hall. The mourners also included another daughter of the deceased Mrs W Travis, Mrs Abraham Hall (Eliza), James and Martha Gilmore, the deceased's sister and her husband, Mr James Gilmore, Mr W Hobson (brother of the deceased) and his wife, Mrs Mary Gilmore and Matilda Hobson, another sister of the murdered woman. Many other relatives also boarded the omnibuses. The cortege left Shelf Street a little before half-past three and slowly moved along Edmund Road, Shoreham Street, Queen's Road, then passed under the railway bridge at Heeley, before climbing the hill to the church, where it arrived at four o'clock. The vicar, the Rev H D Jones was waiting at the gates. All along the route the streets were lined with onlookers. One woman was outraged that Hall had been placed in a cab after the inquest to convey him to the police station, she was heard to say he deserved not only flogging but roasting. By the time the cortege reached the church the crowd was said to number 5000. Detective Wormack and several police officers kept the way clear. The large crowd of onlookers at the church gates remained orderly and showed a dignified interest as the coffin was lifted from the hearse and carried into the church. Only the mourners and press were allowed to attend the service, during which Selina Hall was much affected and her grief aroused considerable commiseration. As the coffin was carried to the graveside Miss Hall was almost prostrate with grief, and had to be supported by her brother and Mr Duckenfield. The grave, a family one, was situated on the hillside in the newer part of the churchyard. The crowd there was particularly large but remained seemly in its conduct. As the vicar read the service for the burial of the dead while the coffin was lowered into the ground, the deceased's son, Abraham, wept bitterly. His sister Selina, now completely overcome, beat her breast hopelessly. When the gravedigger threw soil upon the coffin she called out, 'Oh, my mother, my mother,' and almost fainted. She struggled to the edge of the grave and gazed down at her mother's coffin for the last time. The plaque bore the inscription 'Mary Ann Hall, Died 28th March 1881, aged 48 years'. On the lid was a wreath of daisies and some snowdrops.

Selina Hall's friends thought it expedient to take her from the graveside as soon as possible. As they were escorting her back to the mourning omnibus, which was waiting at the churchyard gates, she fainted, and it was only with great difficulty that she was carried aboard. After the mourners had left the churchyard, a large number of people went to the open grave to take a look at the coffin. Their curiosity having been satisfied, the crowd gradually dwindled away and only the gravedigger remained to carry out his duty.

On 29 April, Hall was removed from his prison cell in Wakefield and taken to Armley Gaol, Leeds. The following day he wrote this letter to his son:

HM Prison, Leeds, 30th April, 1881

Dear son,

I now take the pleasure of writing to inform you that I am removed to Leeds hoping that this will find you quite well as it leaves me as well as can be expected. I inquired at the Town Hall if they had put your mother away and if they put her away in a decent and respectable manner and they said yes and I was glad to hear it and I though that £8 pounds [sic] would be a nice sum to interre [sic] with and to put her away in a respectable manner and I hope her soul is in heaven God bless her and I want you to let me know who was at the Funeral and where they got their tea and who as [sic] took the house and I want you to write on sunday [sic] and then I shall receive it on Monday [sic] and let me know how you all 3 are so I beg to conclude with my kind love to you all and God bless you
From you affectionate father

JAMES HALL
For Abram Hall

No 91 Leadmill road
Sheffield

and I should like to see you on monday [sic] week

James Hall was tried at Leeds Assizes on Friday 6 May, before Mr Justice Kay. Mr Charles Beilby Stuart-Wortley, MP, and Mr Ellis, appeared for the prosecution. Mr Vernon Blackburn and Mr R W Harper conducted the defence. The courtroom was packed and those who knew him well observed that Hall's stay in prison had told severely upon him. However, at the beginning of his trial he gave the appearance of being unconcerned. The prosecution's case was strong and they offered much the same evidence as was heard at the inquest. Several other witnesses were called to give a more comprehensive background with regard to the murdered woman, the prisoner Hall and their family, as well as those directly connected with the events on the night of the murder. As his counsel, Mr Vernon Blackburn, was addressing the jury, Hall gave way to tears. The main thrust of the defence was that at the time his wife was killed, Hall was in a frenzied state of jealousy. He had also been drinking and either the drink or the jealousy, or a combination of both, had produced a state of mind rendering him incapable of knowing what he was doing, or indeed that what he was doing, was wrong, and he had remained in that same state of mind when he spoke to the police. Hall wept throughout the pleas being made on his behalf and continued to cry until his Lordship had finished summing up, during which Mr Justice Kay commented:

> *I hope you will perform your duty with care, deliberation and courage. The statement made before the magistrates by the prisoner is one requiring careful consideration. In it the man made such excuses as he could for the deed, and the excuse he made was that of jealousy. He said he had caught a man in the house with his wife and it is for you to say if there is any foundation for him making that statement. Then was there any reason why he should strike the daughter?...You will have to consider whether the defence is sustainable or not based upon the evidence. It has been argued, and with thought, that the husband was in a frenzied condition of jealousy, that there was an hereditary taint in his blood, that his father had destroyed himself, and that he was not responsible for his actions. But it will not for a moment occur to*

your minds that jealousy, however well founded, could be an excuse for such a crime as this. The question is, not was he jealous or excited by drink; but whether these causes combined to produce such a condition of mind that he did not know the nature or quality of the act he was doing, or if he did know it, that he did not know he was doing wrong. At all events you must not be influenced by any morbid consideration for the prisoner. If you think the prisoner was in a frenzied state of mind, and that he did not know whether he was doing right or wrong, then you can admit the defence; but if you are of the opinion that the evidence does not amount to that, you are bound to find him guilty. I am sure you will consider the case with care and deliberation, as I have tried to put it before you, and that you will consider it courageously, as Englishmen who have a very important duty to perform, both to the prisons and to society.

At 2.55 in the afternoon the jury retired to consider their verdict. They returned at 3.35 and found the prisoner guilty.

When the Clerk of Arraigns asked Hall why sentence of death should not be passed upon him, he replied:

There has been some false witnesses that is all. If I had been allowed to speak I could have contradicted them.

Having assumed the black cap, his Lordship proceeded to pronounce a sentence of death on the prisoner:

Prisoner at the bar, after a very careful inquiry and a very careful attempt to defend you, you have been found guilty of the heinous crime of murder. Your victim was your own wife. I have listened to the evidence with care, and listened in vain for any extenuation. I can give you no hope of mercy in this world. I implore you to use the time left to you, which is short, in trying to make your peace with God. There is mercy there for you, and for the vilest amongst us all. I can but tell you that that is all that is left for you in this world. I am bound to pass upon you the awful sentence of the law. That sentence is that you be taken hence to the place from whence you came, and from thence to the place of execution, and that you be hanged by the neck until you are dead, and that your body shall be buried within the precincts of the prison, and may the Lord have mercy upon your soul.

As Hall was removed from the dock he had once again assumed the appearance of being unconcerned, the same manner that was apparent at the beginning of his trial.

Representations for a reprieve to the Home Secretary by Mr Vernon Blackburn were not successful and the date of execution was set for Monday 23 May. Abraham Hall took a funeral card printed in memory of his mother to his father. On the eve of his execution, along with his final letter to his sister, Sarah, Hall enclosed the card and a request that the verse on his wife's funeral card should also be included on his. In the letter Hall withdrew the charges he had made against his wife:

Dear Sister,

I was glad to receive your letter and to hear that my children have reached home safely and that a lady had been so kind as to ask them to have tea. I hope you will all be able to meet before 8 o'clock tomorrow morning to pray for me the last time on earth. I wish to withdraw my words against my wife. I loved her dearly when I was sober and the sad reason it happened was drunken passion. I hope the Lord Jesus will forgive me for this and all my sins and that you will do the same. Please give my love to Mr and Mrs Allcock; good-bye to sisters, nephews and nieces, to Selina, Abraham and Martha and my last farewell to you all, from your affectionate brother.

JAMES HALL

Abraham, be steady, be steady

Hall requested that the following should be printed as his funeral card:

In Affectionate Remembrance of
JAMES HALL
who departed this life May 23rd 1881
Aged 53 years

> *Farewell, my friends and children dear,*
> *You little thought my time so near,*
> *Grieve not for me, grief is all in vain*
> *Hope in Heaven to meet you all again*

JAMES HALL

The following is part of a report by the journalist who attended Hall's execution from the *Sheffield Daily Telegraph*, which appeared in that newspaper on Tuesday 24 May, the day after the execution:

…At a quarter to eight o'clock Marwood, who arrived at the Gaol on Saturday afternoon and did not leave the building until he had completed his task, entered the condemned cell followed two powerful looking warders. On seeing the executioner with his pinioning straps in his hands, the prisoner raised his arms and uttered 'Oh my God have mercy upon me!' He at once, however, submitted quietly to the pinioning process, which lasted only a few moments. At a few minutes to eight o'clock he was conducted from his cell, and the mournful procession left the corridor and entered the prison yard in the following order; – First came Mr Keane, the governor of the gaol, then Mr Edwin Gray, the under sheriff, and close behind him Marwood and the prisoner, by the side of whom walked two warders ready to render him any assistance if their aid was required. Following these came sixteen other warders who fell in line by the side the scaffold. On emerging from the door of the corridor the culprit came in sight of the scaffold, a high, black mass of wood and calico, erected in a corner of the prison yard, against the hospital, and some thirty or forty yards from the wing in which he had been incarcerated. He started on seeing the erection but soon regained his composure, and walked with an unfaltering step. He paused at the foot of the steps leading to the scaffold, but only for a moment, for at a signal from Marwood, who was by his side, he mounted the stairs with a firm foot and placed himself under the rope, which had previously been fixed by Marwood and hung dangling from the beam above. As the solemn tone of the chaplain reciting the burial service fell upon the ear, Marwood, with a gentle hand, strapped

together the culprit's legs at the ankles. The prisoner was at this time glancing around at the little crowd, composed of the officials and representatives of the Press, in front of him. Beyond a slight tremour on his face he appeared to be perfectly calm, and fully conscious of all that was passing around him. Marwood placed the white cap over the man's face, adjusted the rope, and moved the lever. In another moment there was a loud thud, caused by the falling of the drop, a lesser noise and the culprit had expiated the crime for which he had been condemned. The drop was about nine feet. Mr Wright, who examined the body immediately after the fall, gave it as his opinion that death had been instantaneous, the man's neck having been dislocated by the sudden concussion. Nothing was to be seen but the swaying to and fro of the rope, the body being concealed from view by the black calico covering round the side of the gallows, which was the same erection on which Peace ended his life on the 26th of February, 1879. The body of Hall was allowed to hang the customary hour, and was then taken down…

An inquest was held before the Leeds Borough coroner, Mr Malcolm, at ten' o'clock, at which, the governor of the prison, Mr C A Keane, was first to give evidence.

C A Keane: *I am Governor of this prison…I saw sentence of death carried out. The body now viewed by the jury, is that of James Hall, whom I received on 29th April.*

The surgeon, Mr C J Wright then gave his evidence:

I am a surgeon in Leeds and acting surgeon in this prison. I was present this morning when sentence of death was carried out on James Hall this morning by hanging. I satisfied myself when he was taken down he was dead. The cause of death was strangulation by hanging.

The term 'strangulation by hanging' is an odd one to use, when one considers that Hall supposedly died an instantaneous death. That is according to what the surgeon,

Mr Wright, reportedly told the assembled representatives of the press, as he emerged from beneath the black calico drapes that shielded Hall's body from their view. A 9-foot drop would indicate that Hall's weight was between eight and nine stones, according to the table of drops refined and perfected from Marwood's calculations. Marwood's methods were certainly more successful than most of his predecessors' but he was still refining his long drop technique, which he had introduced when he succeeded William Calcraft as hangman at Newgate in 1874. Marwood would point out to anyone who used the word 'hangman' when referring to himself, that his Calcraft throttled the condemned, whereas he executed them. However, Marwood's method weren't always successful. In May 1878, three years before Hall's execution, Marwood bungled the execution of Vincent Knowles Walker at York, when he gave him too short a drop and Walker died an excruciating death.

The Royal Standard Hotel, *St Mary's Road, where the inquest was held.* The author

CHAPTER 5

The Bath Street Shooting Case

1892

… the man suddenly took hold of the woman by the shawl and fired at her with a revolver.

n Wednesday 8 November 1892, Bath Street, which lies between the Moor and Broomhall Street, was the scene of a sensational shooting case which was initially the source of great mystery and puzzlement. Shortly after six o'clock a man and a woman were seen by Lily Wildgoose, a local resident, and George Waters, who lived at No 3 House, 14 Court, Bath Street, walking arm in arm along the dimly lit street from the direction of Headford Street. When they arrived opposite a wall, behind which was an enclosed yard that was formerly occupied by the Manor Park Dairy Co, the man suddenly took hold of the woman by the shawl and fired at her with a revolver. Leaving the man with her shawl still held tightly in his hand, the woman escaped from his clutches and ran away. Almost immediately the man turned the gun towards himself and with his hand held high fired it into his head. As he fell to the ground, with the shawl under his legs, blood began to flow profusely from his wound. He was still breathing but within a few minutes his body was perfectly still and it was obvious to those who saw him that his life had ebbed away. Lily Wildgoose later told reporters that she saw the man snatch a black lace shawl from his companion and afterwards heard an explosion and saw a flash of fire. The woman screamed and ran away towards Headford Street. Then he turned the gun towards himself and fired another shot. She added that she thought she heard three shots but could only remember seeing two flashes of fire. A young man named George Walters said:

*I was coming home to my tea at six o'clock when I saw a man
and woman. I was coming up Dean Lane and passed them face
to face … I heard three shots and a woman scream. I ran into the
street and saw the man lying on the footpath. He lifted his right
arm up but I should think he was dead within five minutes. When
I saw them they were walking together as if they knew each other
– the same as a man and wife would walk.*

Police Constable Charles Dye was quickly at the scene and
found a six-chamber revolver by the man's side. The body was
removed to the shed in the yard behind the wall before being
transferred to the mortuary. Inspector Stone received some
information regarding the whereabouts of the woman who had
run away from the scene and, about 500 yards from where the
shooting took place, he found her at a shop in Broomhall
Road. She told Inspector Stone that her name was Elizabeth
Baughan and that she had been living at the shop for about a
fortnight. She said she had been out for a walk during the
afternoon and as she was returning home that evening by way
of Bath Street, she heard someone letting off fireworks and
had felt something hit her on the neck. She showed the
inspector a bruise on the left side of her neck and a wound
across her throat. Her landlady said Mrs Baughan had gone
out about 4.30pm and returned a short while after six o'clock,
when she was breathless and almost fainted. When her lodger
went out she was wearing a black shawl but when she came
home she didn't have the shawl with her.

Dr Dunbar was called to examine Mrs Baughan but he
could find no gunshot injuries. The wounds she had sustained
to her neck were only slight. When the inspector asked Mrs
Baughan about her shawl she said that she was wearing it
when she went out but she couldn't remember if she still had
it round her neck when the 'fireworks' went off. She said she
thought she had dropped it as she hurried home. Her answers
were vague and she appeared to be in a somewhat dazed
condition. The following day details of the strange events in
Bath Street were published in the newspapers, as well as a full
description of the deceased, a yet unidentified man.

The *Sheffield And Rotherham Independent* reported on
Thursday 10 November:

William Curtis shoots himself in Bath Street as a distraught Elizabeth Baughan flees the scene. Author's collection

A good deal of mystery which was associated with the attempted murder and suicide in Bath street on Tuesday night has now been cleared up. The body of the man who attempted to shoot Mrs Baughan, and then destroyed himself by discharging a revolver at his head, was identified early yesterday morning. Information was also forthcoming during the day which sheds light on the relations which have existed between the man and the woman, and which formulated a probable clue for the motive of the crime. The body was identified by Mr Henry Curtis, a forgeman employed at Messrs Jessop's Works, at Brightside, as that of his father, William Curtis, a master forgeman engaged at the same establishment, and who resided at Rosehill, Brightside Village. Mr Henry Curtis saw an account of the occurrence in the morning papers, and learning that his father had not returned

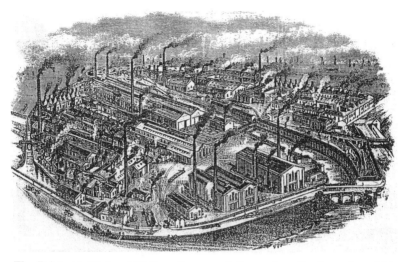

The Brightside Works of William Jessop and Sons where Curtis conducted his successful business as a Master Forgeman. Author's collection

home, on the previous night, he proceeded to the mortuary, and had no difficulty in recognising the body.

The wounds on Mrs Baughan's neck were understood to have been caused when her shawl was forcibly ripped from her neck. A large bone pin believed to have fastened it was found at the scene of the shooting on 9 November.

Once the dead man's identity was known it did not take long to discover that there had been a long course of intimacy between himself and Mrs Baughan. It transpired that William Curtis had been living in the Brightside area for about twelve years. He was a man in comfortable circumstances, who as a master forgeman, working out of the Brightside Works, had several men in his employ, including his two sons, and was in receipt of a comparatively good income. He was greatly respected and looked up to by his neighbours. He had two sons and a daughter from his first marriage, who were all married themselves. He had remarried. There was a scandal in the area following one of Mr Curtis' sons seeing his father and Mrs Baughan together when he had assaulted them both in the street; and Mrs Baughan had subsequently brought charges, the young man receiving a fine for the assault. The assault did nothing to prevent Mr Curtis and Mrs Baughan continuing their association.

Mrs Baughan, who was aged about thirty, was also well thought of in the area. Her former neighbours in Jenkins Street described her as a prepossessing, well-dressed woman who, following her husband's death, had followed no occupation. However, it was understood that she received money and goods from her mother, who lived in Chester. A fortnight before the incident in Bath Street, Mrs Baughan had told her neighbours that she was leaving Sheffield to go and live with her mother and sister, who were both invalids. Her household goods had been packed away in crates and Mrs Baughan moved out of the house. On Friday 4 November the crates and furniture had been collected in a cart to be taken to Chester. Following the shooting Mrs Baughan removed herself from her temporary lodgings in Broomhall to her married brothers house at Pitsmoor.

The inquest was opened and adjourned on Thursday 10 November at Sheffield Mortuary, in Plum Lane, before coroner Dossey Wightman, Esquire.

Mrs Bessie Curtis said:

I am the widow of the deceased. He was fifty-five years of age and a forgeman. I have lived with him at No 11 Burslem Street, Brightside. I last saw him alive on Tuesday about ten minutes to one o'clock. He left Brightside by the ten minutes to two train, as I thought, for Sheffield. He had a revolver with him, but he was not in the habit of carrying one. I think he had it about a fortnight. He showed it to me on Monday night. I was not sure whether he had one before Monday night, but I think he had, as he told me not to feel in his pocket. He told me he had borrowed it. I have seen the body here; it is that of my husband.

Mr Wightman said:

There is some difficulty with this case. We are here simply for the purpose of having the body identified prior to a post-mortem being made, and also for the purpose of giving a burial certificate. At the time I received the report of this death there was little or nothing known about the deceased; and accordingly ordered an inquest for this morning, with the intention of adjourning until more was known about the deceased... There must be a post-mortem examination, as I do not know whether the man shot himself or was shot by someone else. Both are probable but the post-mortem examination will show which is the most reasonable.

Mr Wightman then adjourned the inquest until the following Wednesday afternoon. At the conclusion of the hearing, Mr A Muir Wilson was retained by the deceased's family.

The remains of William Henry Curtis were interred in Grimesthorpe churchyard on Saturday 12 November. A large crowd had assembled outside the church. Many of Curtis' workmates from Messrs Jessop's Works at Brightside were in attendance, as were a large contingency from Brightside Conservative Club. The coffin, which was of polished cherry wood, was made by Messrs Jessop & Sons and was borne into the church and afterwards to the grave by six of the deceased's workmates. The service was conducted by the Rev William Sykes, curate of Carbrook Church and the chief mourners were Mrs Bessie Curtis (widow), Mr Henry Curtis and Mr Albert Curtis, sons of the deceased and Mr Harvey Curtis, brother of the deceased.

The inquest was resumed at Sheffield Mortuary before coroner Dossey Wightman, Esquire, on Wednesday 17 November at 4pm. Several of the deceased's family were present. Some of them gave evidence tinged with tones of strong feeling against Mrs Baughan.

Mr Arthur Hallam, police surgeon, said he made a post-mortem examination on the body of William Curtis on 10 November. He found a large contused wound on the back of the hand, probably caused by falling. Also a gunshot wound in the back part of the roof of the mouth, the shot having apparently entered from the front. The lips and teeth were not injured. He traced the wound through the base of the skull, out of the temporal bone, and along the muscles of the neck. The splintered bones had been forced into the brain substance. He did not discover the shot, which must have gone right through the head. With such a wound the man could not live more than ten minutes. Judging by the position of the wound it must have been self-inflicted. It was almost impossible for a second party to have done it. There was nothing in connection with the brain that would indicate the state of the man's mind.

When called to give her evidence, Mrs Baughan was dressed in mourning and wore a wrapper round her throat. She was still suffering from the injuries.

Elizabeth B: *I am the widow of William Baughan who lived at Brightside and was a brick setter. He died twelve months ago last April. I continued to live at the house until three weeks ago. I have known William Henry Curtis a number of years – I dare say ten years. He lived in Burslem Street, Brightside and was a foreman. I don't know his age.*

The coroner: *You have been in the habit of seeing him sometimes?*

Elizabeth B: *Yes.*

The coroner: *Is he a married man?*

Elizabeth B: *I think so.*

The coroner: *You know he is, don't you, now?*

Elizabeth B: *Yes, I do.*

The coroner: *If you answer the questions honestly I will not take any advantage of you, nor trouble you any more than I can help.*

Elizabeth B: *I have for three weeks been staying with friends in Darnall, Pitsmoor, and Broomhall Street, and I went to Broomhall Street a week before the occurrence. I went to stay with my friend, Elizabeth Wheatley, a widow. I saw the deceased most days after going to Broomhall Street. I usually met him in the street, I never met him by appointment. I had met him frequently for some weeks previously. I have never lived with him; not even for a day or night. On the day of the occurrence I met him between four and five o'clock in Division Street. I had no appointment to meet him there. I saw him on the previous meeting but he did not then make an appointment, nor did I. On Tuesday night he came up behind and overtook me in Division Street, and asked me where I was going. I said I was having a walk. He did not speak, but walked by my side along Division Street in silence. He asked me to go somewhere as he wanted to talk. We went to a public house somewhere off Division Street. I don't know the name of the house. It is off Eldon Street, I think. We stayed about three-quarters of an hour and then left. I went down Bath Street, and he left me. I thought he had gone home, but he must have followed me. He scarcely spoke three words in the public house. He had two glasses of beer. I went along Bath Street not knowing until I reached the end that there was no outlet. I wanted to get into Broomhall Street, but made a mistake in not turning out of Bath Street. I did not know he was following me. I don't remember anything until somebody clutched my throat and fired. I did not see who it was. I had just got in sight of the blank wall and was turning round to go back when I suddenly felt someone clutch at my throat, and I saw some fire flashing. I thought at the time it was fireworks. I felt a burning at the throat at the time. I certainly did not see Curtis at all, even when I was seized. I really did not know what I was doing just then. I did not see a man running away. There had been no quarrel in the public house. He asked me if I intended going away. I said yes, and he did not reply. I had told him on the money that I was going, when he tried to persuade me not to go away. He had tried to persuade me many times. He has never threatened me at all. He has never contributed to my support. He never gave me money at any time.*

The coroner: *Did he offer to go away with you?*

Elizabeth B: *Yes; but I refused. He did not want to go with me where I was going then.*

The coroner: *Has he ever wanted you to go away with him?*

Elizabeth B: *Yes.*

The coroner: *Have you ever been in difficulty with regard to money matters?*

Elizabeth B: *No.*

The coroner: *Never applied to him for assistance?*

Elizabeth B: *I have asked him; he never gave me anything.*

The coroner: *Have you ever been to his house?*

Elizabeth B: *Never.*

The coroner: *Did you know his wife?*

Elizabeth B: *By sight only.*

The coroner: *There has never been any quarrel or discussion between you and Curtis's wife?*

Elizabeth B: *No.*

Mr Wilson then rose as he wished to cross-examine the witness, during the course of which Mrs Baughan reiterated some of her previous evidence she told him.

Elizabeth B: *I have known the deceased for about ten years. I cannot say how I made his acquaintance. I was then living in Thomas Street, Brightside. His first wife was living then.*

Mr Wilson: *Did he go to your house?*

Elizabeth B: *He used to visit my husband; he did not visit me.*

Mr Wilson: *Has he been there when your husband was out?*

Elizabeth B: *No, never.*

Mr Wilson: *Have you ever walked out with him during his first wife's life?*

Elizabeth B: *Yes.*

Elizabeth B: *Where did you go?*

Mr Wilson: *I could not tell you where, but I have walked out with him.*

Mr Wilson: *When his first wife died did he still continue coming to the house?*

Elizabeth B: *No, he did not.*

Mr Wilson: *When he got married a second time did he come?*

Elizabeth B: *He has occasionally been.*

Mr Wilson: *To see your husband?*

Elizabeth B: *He came to see him.*

Mr Wilson: *After your husband's death did he still continue to come?*

Elizabeth B: *He came one or twice.*

Mr Wilson: *To see your husband then?*

Elizabeth B: *To see me. I cannot tell you how many times he has been. I never knew when he was coming. He used to come in when I did not know he was coming.*

Mr Wilson: *Once a week at least?*

Elizabeth B: *No, nor once a month.*

Mr Wilson: *Frequently?*

Elizabeth B: *No, he did not come frequently. He might have been half-a-dozen times since my husband's death.*

Mr Wilson: *How many times have you walked out with him since your husband's death?*

Elizabeth B: *I could not say. Many times.*

Mr Wilson: *Was he keeping company with you?*

The coroner: *When they walked out together, it looked like it.*

Mr Wilson: *It does – a married man and a widow.*

Elizabeth B: *He used to stay half-an-hour or so, or only a few minutes many a time. Mrs Wheatley, with whom I was staying in Broomhall Street, is a friend of mine. I swear that I did not take any furniture there; I took my box. I have seen him come and wait about outside there.*

The coroner: *I do not wish to stop Mr Wilson, because it is my duty to sift the substance to the bottom. I think the questions will only lead to the conclusion which I think all of us here have probably already come to*

– that there was a connection, illicit or otherwise, between this woman and the deceased.

Mr Wilson: *If the witness will admit it, frankly, there will be an end of it. I want to show what was operating on this man's mind to induce him to do what he did. I am trying to show that there was an adulterous connection between them.*

The coroner: *That is a step further than I had indicated. I suggest Mr Wilson that you continue with your questioning of this witness.*

Mr Wilson: *I will say it plainly – has this man ever committed himself with you? You can answer it or not as you please, yes or no?*

The coroner: *You will do yourself by answering the question in a straightforward and honest manner. You are in a very nasty position, and would do well to speak the truth.* [In exasperation] *If there has been a connection let her admit it; if not, let her say never and not force Mr Wilson's questions.*

Mr Wilson: *Now, was there?*

The witness simply hung down her head and would not reply.

The coroner: *I think Mr Wilson you make take your answer in the witness's silence, as I, and the jury will.*

Mrs Baughan replied to further questions that were put to her and denied that there had been a quarrel between herself and the deceased when they had met in the afternoon. She said she did not know that he had any weapon with him and that he did not say that day he would kill himself if she went away. He had said some time ago that he would make an end of it. Mr Wilson continued to put further questions to Mrs Baughan, the purpose of which was questioned by a member of the jury, to which the coroner replied:

Our duty is to ascertain how this man came by his death. The main question is, who shot him, and therefore Mr Wilson is justified in seeking to elicit information on that point.

Mr Wilson: *That is what I wish this woman to say.*

Juryman: *It seems to be nothing but a lot of cross-questioning.*

Mr Wilson: *It is not for you to interrupt.*

The coroner: *I wish to give Mr Wilson all the liberty in my power with the object of showing that there is no possibility of anyone else having shot the deceased.*

After several more questions had been put to her by Mr Wilson, Mrs Baughan stepped down.

Further witnesses were called to give their version of what they saw on the night of the shooting. In his summing up the coroner said to the jury:

I think in all probability you have come to the same conclusion that I have, that there has been a connection of some kind – you can form your own opinion as to its nature, between Mrs Baughan and the deceased. According to her own evidence they had been keeping company for a considerable time. She swore that there was no quarrel between them on this afternoon, but she admitted that he said if she did go there would be an end of it. Of what that might mean you must form your own opinion. Singularly enough, there is no evidence of any quarrel, either in the house or in the street. The question for you to decide, first of all, which you will have no trouble about, is how the man met his death? It is quite clear he met his death by being shot. The next question is, who shot him? There is no evidence, nor, so far as I know, any imputation or suspicion that the woman shot him. You are not bound by any opinion of mine, but if I had to pass one, I should say that the probable explanation of the whole thing was that here was a married man who had got an infatuation for, or at any rate an intimacy with this woman, and because she was going away he was determined to shoot her first and himself afterwards, and that he missed her and hit himself.

The jury returned a verdict of 'suicide'. The coroner then asked the jury's opinion as to the deceased's state of mind and hinted that they might like to give the deceased the benefit of the doubt. Accordingly the jury returned a verdict of 'suicide while in a state of temporary insanity,' which the coroner duly recorded.

Mrs Baughan left the proceedings during the coroner's summing up and the deceased's son and several other relatives followed her. There was some strong language and scuffling on the stairs as Mrs Baughan attempted to leave the mortuary building. It became necessary for the police to intervene and to take Mrs Baughan away; and she was given refuge in a neighbouring shed. She remained there until it was considered safe so she might leave without fear of disturbance.

St Thomas's Church, Grimesthorpe, where William Curtis' funeral was held and where he lies buried in the churchyard. The author

CHAPTER 6

Suicides

1892

During the period when suicide was regarded as a criminal act, failed suicides were often hanged afterwards. Although by the closing years of the nineteenth century suicide was being treated more sympathetically than earlier in the century, when it was common for the Church to refuse burial of a suicide victim (or self-murderer as some would have it) in consecrated ground. The origins of this practice are vested in pre-empting the vengeance of the suicide's ghost on those who had driven the person to the act. Various acts of indignity were sometimes inflicted on the corpse, such as cutting off the right hand to render its ghost less formidable. The theory was that a stake being driven through the heart would prevent the ghost from 'walking'. The additional protection of burying a suicide at a crossroads would be sure to confuse a malevolent spirit about direction. The last such burial took place in London at the junction of Grosvenor Place and the Kings Road, Chelsea, when a man named Griffiths was buried there in 1823. That same year parliament passed an Act allowing burials in churchyards, a move instigated by King George IV, who had been delayed by such a burial. The church continued to take a dim view of suicides and their burials were usually confined to out of the way places or 'suicides corner', internment normally taking place at night between the hours of nine o'clock and midnight, without any form of religious ceremony.

In Acts of Parliament passed in 1879 and 1882, suicide ceased to be legally regarded as homicide and burial during daylight hours was allowed. Many members of the clergy still

Dossey Wightman (1836–1920), solicitor and partner of the Sheffield firm Wightman and Parker, of Exchange Court. He was coroner from 1873–1911. Author's collection

regarded suicide as a disgraceful act, and refused to have anything to do with burials. Others would sometimes conduct a church funeral service for the deceased person within the church for the sake of the family, while the coffin either remained outside the building or within the porch. My mother told me of such a funeral, only ten miles or so from Sheffield city centre, which took place as late as the 1950s. Often, after 1882, when suicides were buried within a churchyard, the practice of burial without any form of religious ceremony continued. From 1873–1911, Sheffield was blessed with a sympathetic coroner, Dossey Wightman (1836–1920), who was involved with the cases featured here. Mr Wightman would indicate to juries, whenever he saw the slightest opportunity, that they might give the deceased the benefit of the doubt by bringing in a verdict of 'suicide while of unsound mind' or 'suicide during temporary insanity', or a similar verdict. The inclusion of these epithets would not only help to soften the blow to the families of suicides but also to de-stigmatize the act to many more conservative citizens. It was not until 1961 that suicide was finally decriminalised. In more recent times the term 'committed suicide' is less widely used, as the prefix commit is interpreted by some as still being suggestive of a criminal act. The sadness and tragedy that invariably surrounds such cases remains an imponderable obstacle for those left behind.

Medically Discharged Soldier Shoots Himself

… he behaved in what Mrs Dunkley described as being a 'rough and peculiar' manner.

Twenty-three-year-old James Mann, who lived with his parents at 77 Channing Street, Walkley, had been discharged from the army following an injury to his right ankle, received when he had fallen from a ladder while cleaning a barrack window. Following his discharge he had been receiving a pension of 10*d.* a day, which he supplemented by working as a filecutter. For fifteen months he had courted a widow, Mrs Ellen Eliza Dunkley, who lived in Balaclava Road, and they were due to marry in a fortnight. He worked alongside a neighbour, Joseph Drabble, who lived at 75 Channing Road, to whom he often complained of severe pain in his right ankle. On Friday 12 February, Mann told his mother that the pain was so severe that it made him tired of living.

Mann would occasionally binge drink, as the drink would help to numb the pain in his ankle. Unfortunately the wrong combination of alcohol could sometimes induce him to become violent. This was the case on the evening of Saturday 13 February, when he was in the company of his fiancée from 7.15pm until 10.30pm. He behaved in what Mrs Dunkley described as a 'rough and peculiar' manner. The couple argued and Mann seized hold of Mrs Dunkley, who told him to go away and never come again. She said later that if someone hadn't come in and disturbed them, she believed that her fiancée would have killed her. Mann arrived back at his parents' house about 11.30pm. Mr and Mrs Mann had gone to bed. On hearing her son arrive home, Mrs Mann waited a few moments then called out from her bedroom to ask if he had found his supper. He replied that he had, in a voice that his mother later described as 'broken' – as though he was crying. She heard him go into the room at the front of the house, return through the kitchen and leave by the back door into the yard.

It seems that Mann went into the front room and picked up his father's two-barrelled, breech-loading shotgun. He then went to the kitchen and took two cartridges from the top shelf and loaded the gun, before leaving the house. The next thing that was heard was the loud report of a single gunshot. When Mrs Mann rushed to a back bedroom window, she saw her son lying at the top of the yard. Mann's workmate and neighbour Joseph Drabble, had also heard the report. He ran downstairs into the yard. On seeing what had occurred he went to fetch the police. Sergeant Yardley went up to Mann's body and saw that he had blown away his face and the top of his head, and had either put the barrel of the gun into his mouth or under his chin. It was later discovered that only the right-hand barrel had been discharged.

Depressed Cutlery Manufacturer Cuts His Throat

… saw him kneeling down with a razor in each hand with which he was cutting his throat.

On Monday 15 February, Frederick Gray, a forty-year-old unmarried cutlery manufacturer, in business with his brother in Clarence Street, who lived with his spinster sister in Weston Street, committed suicide by cutting his throat with a razor. Mr Gray had been receiving treatment for the previous three months from Dr Keeling, for a nervous debility, which had resulted in his extreme depression. As a result of his depressed state Mr Gray had been closely watched and such were his family's concerns that all objects with which he might harm himself had been removed from his reach, or so it was believed. Early on the morning of the day of his death Mr Gray went to his brother's house and roused him from bed. His manner was very strange and his brother accompanied him back home and remained with him throughout the day. At about six o'clock in the evening Mr Gray told his brother that he felt very hot. He then went upstairs and into his bedroom, which was in darkness. His brother followed him and on entering the bedroom saw him kneeling down with a razor in each hand with which he was cutting his throat. A struggle ensued and as Mr Gray's brother tried to wrest the razors from his hands, received several cuts to his own hands. Dr Sinclair

White and Mr Nadin, a surgeon, who both lived locally, were sent for but it was too late to administer any medical assistance to Mr Gray, as he had severed his windpipe and had already expired. Exactly where the deceased had got the razors was a mystery to both his brother and sister, as he did not shave. It was supposed that Mr Gray must have obtained the razors for the purpose of committing suicide sometime previously and secreted them in his bedroom.

Shocking Death of Well-Known Sheffield Merchant

... stretched across the floor surrounded by a large pool of blood, which had soaked into the carpet.

Many Sheffield residents were sorry to read the shocking news in the newspapers that Mr George Langley, a well-known fish and game salesman, oyster merchant and wholesale shellfish merchant, who resided at No 1 Baker's Hill, had been found dead, brought about by his own hand. Fifty-three-year-old Mr Langley, traded from the Shambles end of the wholesale Sheaf Market. For several years Mr Langley had been addicted to intoxicating liquor and, in the seven weeks or so since Christmas time, had been indulging himself in strong drink to excess. For two or three days Mr Langley had remained at home in an attempt to cure himself of the accumulated effect of his debauchery. This had, however, only served to make him despondent and those who had seen him said he had a strange look in his eyes. On Tuesday 16 February, Mr Langley remained in bed all day. He got up in the evening and went to the kitchen, where Mr and Mrs William Downing, who lived in the same house, were sitting and just about to retire to bed. Mr and Mrs Downing left Mr Langley drinking brandy and water, and noticed that he seemed a little more cheerful. The Downing's bedroom was on the top storey of the house, Mr Langley's on the first floor, below.

At about 5am the following morning Mrs Downing felt thirsty and went downstairs for some water. As she passed Mr Langley's bedroom door she noticed that the gaslight was full on. As this was somewhat unusual at such an hour, and as the door was slightly ajar, she looked into the bedroom. Mr Langley was stretched across the floor surrounded by a large pool of blood, which had soaked into the carpet. There was a deep gash across his throat and a carving knife lay nearby. What remained of the brandy and water that Mr Langley had been drinking when last seen by Mr and Mrs Downing was in a glass on the dressing table. Mrs Gowning ran upstairs to inform her husband, who went out of the house and fetched a neighbour, Mrs Keeton, before bringing back police constables Ashton and Foster to the house. Mr Langley was beyond help as he had been dead for several hours. The deceased had onetime lived at No 3 Baker's Hill before removing to No 1 following the breakdown of his marriage over ten years previously. Only six months before, while suffering from the effects of drink, Mr Langley had tried to cut his throat with the same knife and had only been prevented from doing so by the opportune intervention of the Downings.

Depressed Publican's Suicide

… seemed much troubled recently and had been drinking heavily for several weeks …

On Sunday 28 February, the landlord of the *Victoria Hotel*, situated in Neepsend Lane, was found in the hayloft above the stable at the back of his premises, with his throat cut and a razor lying by his side. Publican Francis Broadbent, had seemed much troubled recently and had been drinking heavily for several weeks, his principal tipple being whisky. On Saturday night, following a heavy drinking session, Mr Broadbent went to bed at about 11.30pm. He slept alone, his wife occupying another bedroom. At 8am on Sunday morning Mrs Broadbent heard her husband get up and go downstairs. A female relative was in the kitchen at the time and saw Mr Broadbent go outside. A short while later Mrs Broadbent came down to breakfast and when her husband didn't appear for his breakfast a search was made for him, but he could not be found. Later that morning John Riches, who lived nearby in Fairfield Road, noticed a pool of blood emanating from within the stable where Mr Broadbent's body was subsequently found in the hayloft.

Found Drowned in Endcliffe Dam

… there was nothing in her manner to arouse his suspicion.

On Tuesday 19 April, Elizabeth Bell's body was found floating in the bathing dam at Endcliffe. Mrs Bell had been temporarily living alone in Egerton Street West for the previous few days, while her husband, George, a cowkeeper, remained at their former home at 56 Bowdon Street, while he gradually prepared the rooms in Egerton Street to receive the furniture. At the inquest held at Sheffield Mortuary before coroner Dossey Wightman, Esquire, the following day, it was revealed that the tragic death of the Bell's daughter some twelve months previously had prayed heavily on Mrs Bell's mind; and the recent news that her son-in-law was to remarry had greatly saddened her. Mr Bell said that his wife habitually took walks through Endcliffe Woods. He added that he had last seen his wife alive on Monday afternoon and that there was nothing in her manner to arouse his suspicion. He added that he believed she had committed suicide and that the

Endcliffe Dam, where Elizabeth Bell's body was found floating, on Tuesday 19 April 1892. Author's collection

distress caused by their daughter's death and the news of the forthcoming marriage had induced her to do so. Mr Wightman said there was not so much evidence in this case as there usually was, to show the state of mind of the deceased when she threw herself into the water. The jury's verdict was 'committed suicide while in a state of temporary insanity'.

Young Woodcarver Found Hanged at Home

…found him hanging from the banisters, suspended by means of a muffler, with which he had fashioned a makeshift noose.

On the morning of Thursday 28 April, William Durrant, aged twenty-one, a woodcarver, was found dead, having hanged himself at the home he shared with his parents at 52 Russell Street, Westbar. The dead man worked for Mr Crowther, a cabinetmaker who operated from business premises in Brown Street. For five or six weeks prior to his death he had been unwell, which caused him to be severely depressed, although he had apparently never threatened to take his own life, nor had he led his parents to believe that might be his intention. On the morning of his death he got up as usual and ate his breakfast. His mother said there was nothing unusual in his manner, as he bade her good morning and went out as if he was going to work. Later in the morning she found him hanging from the banisters, suspended by means of a muffler, with which he had fashioned a makeshift noose. The evidence presented at the inquest indicated that the deceased had taken his own life in consequence of his ill health, prompting the jury to return a verdict that William Nathanial Durrant had committed suicide while in a state of temporary insanity.

Slackness of Business Prompts Publican's Suicide

…he had a six-chambered revolver in his hand, from which he had discharged one bullet, having shot himself in the head.

On Saturday 7 May, thirty-six-year-old George Swinden, an edge tool striker and landlord of the *Crooked Billet*, Scotland

Street, returned home at 1.00pm from work and complained to his wife, Emma, that he was feeling tired. He ate his dinner then went upstairs to bed. Mr Swinden had been in low spirits for more than three weeks, as business had been very slack. In fact as business had not been good for quite some time, to supplement his income from the public house, it had become necessary to fall back on his old job as an edge tool maker. Recently the slackness of trade in both his enterprises had caused him considerable worries. Shortly after six o'clock that evening Mrs Swinden sent her son upstairs to wake his father for his tea. She was surprised when her son returned and told her that the bedroom door was locked and he had got no reply. She went to investigate herself and was alarmed when Mr Swinden called out to her in a weak and feeble voice. She fetched two men who were drinking in the bar and they broke down the door. When the door burst open Mr Swinden was found lying on the bed, with a six-chambered revolver in his right hand, from which he had discharged one bullet. He had shot himself in the head and the bullet had entered through the right temple. Barely alive, Mr Swinden was taken to the Infirmary after he had been attended to by a surgeon, Mr Rhymes of St James' Street. While doctors attempted to save his life they indicated to Mrs Swinden that such were her husband's injuries that his recovery was unlikely, as the bullet had lodged in his brain. He died in the early hours of Sunday morning. The inquest was held at the Infirmary on Tuesday 10 May before coroner Dossey Wightman, Esquire, where it was heard that the deceased had never threatened to commit suicide. The jury returned a verdict of 'suicide during a state of temporary insanity'.

Death in Button Lane

This once very active woman had become a mere shadow of her former self…

Maria Topham was in business as a fish dealer and herring curer. She lived at 62 Button Lane, with her son and daughter. She had been unwell for several months and had been receiving medical attention. Such was her poor state of health that she needed frequent nursing care. Her son and daughter took care of her daytime needs and a young woman who lived locally provided nursing care at night. This once very active woman had become a mere shadow of her former self and this caused her great distress. At three o'clock in the morning of Wednesday 22 June, the girl give Mrs Topham some medicine. She then left the room for a short time. When she came back she found that Mrs Topham was not in bed and had in fact left the bedroom. On going downstairs she found Maria Topham in the downstairs living room near the fireplace, lying on the floor, with her throat cut and a bloodstained razor nearby. Dr France was sent for but Mrs Topham was dead before he arrived.

Man Found Hanged in Scaithe Wood

He hadn't worked during the time he had been ill and it had preyed on his mind.

On the evening of Tuesday 13 July, some children were playing in Scaithe Wood, adjoining the Park Wood at Wadsley Bridge. As they were running along the paths enjoying the pleasant evening air, they came across the body of a man hanging from a tree. They immediately left the wood and informed the police. Police Constable Reynolds, taking some civilian help with him, was shown the location of the tree by the children and the man's body was subsequently cut down and conveyed to the *Gate Inn*, Wadsley Bridge. The body was identified as that of forty-four-year-old Jonathan Alderson, who lived at 15 Whitehouse Lane, with his wife and two children. Mr Alderson had been suffering from a nervous debility for between four and five months and was being treated by Dr Hodgson. He hadn't worked during the time he had been ill and it had preyed on his mind. Early that morning he had gone out saying that he was going to look for some work and he was last seen alive about seven o'clock that evening walking near the wood. When he was found hanging from a rope he had suspended from a tree branch, his feet were just a few inches from the ground.

Tragic Death of Father of Seven

… said that her husband had been unwell for some time and had been troubled about something.

On Saturday 16 July, forty-six-year-old George Henry Hamer, Inspector of Canal Boats for Sheffield Corporation, was found floating in the canal near Attercliffe Station. Mr Hamer's hat and coat were found nearby on the canal bank. Police Constable Curtis was summoned and the body was recovered and conveyed to the deceased's house at No 44 Bawtry Road. Mr Hamer, the father of seven children, had not been seen since he had left his home the previous morning. The inquest was held on Monday 18 July before coroner Dossey Wightman, Esquire, at the *Sportsman's Inn*, Darnall. Mrs Hamer said that her husband had been unwell for some time and had been troubled about something. On Thursday night he was unusually quiet and hardly spoke to his family. The next morning he had left the house and was not seen again until his body had been discovered floating in the canal. A note written in a pocketbook found in one of the pockets of his coat read:

My Dear Tet,
Forgive me, the remnant of a misspent life and a broken-hearted. Think of what I am and what I might have been, and made thee. God bless you and my dear, dear children. Yours without hope,

George

PS

You have been too good for me, dearest; I cannot express myself…

The postscript mentioned sending his love to his children and also referred to some monetary affairs, before concluding:

… Ask Bob and Gordon never to touch drink or gambling, and forgive me. There is more on my mind than I can bear. Don't call

me a coward. Give my love to the Revs. R. C. Jeynt, G. G. Swann, Mr Calvert, and Mr Gutteridge.

After a short deliberation, the foreman of the jury rose and returned a verdict that Mr Hamer committed suicide, before adding that they had also concluded that he was of unsound mind at the time.

Found Hanging by His Belt in Spital Hill

He hadn't worked for several months and became very despondent as a result.

Fifty-four-year-old labourer Jabez Guy lived in Sorby Street, Spital Hill. He hadn't worked for several months and became very despondent as a result. Three years before he had made a final attempt to take his own life, he had only been prevented from succeeding in doing so by the timely intervention of his wife. On Wednesday 20 July, Mr Guy rose early. At 5.30am he told his wife he was going out to find work. Two hours later, when Mrs Guy got up herself, she discovered her husband hanging by his belt, from the banisters leading to the attic. She cut him down but it was too late, as he was already dead. Unfortunately she had been unable to save his life a second time.

Woman's Body Found Floating in Dam at Sharrow Vale

… had threatened to commit suicide on several occasions.

Early on the morning of Wednesday 3 August, James Firth, an engine tenter, employed at the Lower Snuff Mill, Sharrow Vale, found a woman's body floating in the dam there. He informed the police and with the assistance of Sergeant Platts, Mr Firth was able to recover the woman's body from the water. The dead woman was identified as Mrs Ann Ford of 28 Ashley Road. Mrs Ford had been in a state of melancholia for some time and subject to prolonged periods of despondency. In recent months she had threatened to commit suicide on several occasions. Mr Luke Ford, her husband, and a small party of friends had been searching for her since the previous evening and all through the night, after she hadn't returned home.

Drowned at Loxley

… on several occasions, when he had been in particularly low spirits, he had threatened to commit suicide.

Seventy-nine-year-old gardener Thomas Blakey lived with his son-in-law at Loxley. Mr Blakey had been in low spirits for a considerable time and was subject to periodic bouts of severe depression. Such was the depth of his despondency that on several occasions when he had been in particularly low spirits he had threatened to commit suicide. On Saturday 13 August, when Mr Blakey left home, he showed no unusual signs in his manner. At about five o'clock in the afternoon two children saw him standing by the water's edge at Ashton Carr Dam, Loxley, at a place where the water was about 20ft deep. Shortly afterwards they heard someone calling out and when they went to investigate the children saw that Mr Blakey was in the water. They ran for help and a man named Joseph Hague arrived quickly at the scene, followed shortly afterwards by Police Constable Hedland. Mr Blakey's body was soon brought to the bank but despite prompt medical attention being administered, the old man could not be resuscitated.

Found Hanged in a Nether Edge Garden

… he was suspended from the clothes post by means of a cord that had been attached round his neck.

Mr George Herbert Tasker of the Sheffield firm Messrs. Roper and Tasker, toy and smallware dealers of Pinstone Street, lived with his family at No 14, Ashland Road, Nether Edge. At about 7.30am on Thursday 18 August, the gardener, John Oldfield, noticed a man apparently leaning against a clothes post in the garden and gazing upwards. Mr Oldfield thought no more of it and carried on with his work. Fifteen minutes or so later a newsagent named Smith was passing by and also noticed the motionless man standing by the clothes post and remarked to the gardener that it was very singular. The two men then went up to the clothes post and discovered the man was Mr Isaac Roper, the seventy-five-year-old father-in-law of Mr Tasker, and much to their horror that he was suspended from the clothes post by means of a cord that had been attached round his neck. Mr Oldfield at once cut the cord by means of his pruning knife but it soon became apparent that not only was Mr Roper dead but that he had been so for several hours. Before he had been cut down Mr Roper's feet were on the ground and it was supposed that he had strangled himself by tying the cord round his neck and leaning forward.

On the previous night the family had retired leaving a servant to finish her work. She heard Mr Roper come downstairs about 1.00am and go out. The girl finished her work and went to bed. It seems Mr Roper had hanged himself shortly after he had gone out.

Formerly the senior partner in the firm of Roper and Tasker, Mr Roper was well placed financially. He had suffered a stroke in November 1991, since when he had been in a very poor state of health. His eyesight was bad and he complained of head pains and insomnia. His family said these medical problems seemed to pray on his mind and in the weeks leading up to his death he had been in a constant state of restlessness and low spirits.

Carter Delirious with Pain Cuts his Throat

… saw her brother in the act of cutting his throat with a razor.

William Pratt, a forty-year-old carter, lived with his sister at No 15 Ward Street. Towards the end of August, Mr Pratt had fallen from a cart that was in his charge and broken one of his ribs. He was attended by a doctor, but during the days that followed, inflammation set in and caused him considerable pain. The pain eventually became so bad that he became delirious. On the morning of Monday 12 September, Mr Pratt went into his bedroom. His sister heard him call out in pain. She went into his room and saw her brother in the act of cutting his throat with a razor. She ran to fetch help and Mr Pratt was conveyed to the Infirmary in an ambulance. He died within half an hour of being admitted. At the inquest held at the Infirmary before coroner Dossey Wightman, Esquire, on 13 September, the jury returned a verdict of 'suicide while temporary insane'.

Unemployed Labourer Found Dying in Adelphi Street

She was alarmed to see that the blood was actually flowing onto the step from under the door.

Labourer George Poole lived with his wife and four young children in Adelphi Street. He had been in low spirits for some time as he had been out of work and despite making every effort to find employment he had not been successful. On the morning of Wednesday 10 November, his wife took one of their children to the Children's Hospital in Western Bank. While she was out her husband took his own life. Sarah Hague, a young woman who also lived in Adelphi Street, was passing the Poole's house when she noticed some blood on the doorstep. She was alarmed to see that the blood was actually flowing onto the step from under the door. Curious to find out where the blood was coming from, she pushed the door open and was confronted by her neighbour, George Poole, who was lying on the floor, with his throat cut and a bloodstained pocket-knife lying open by his side. He was still alive but continued to lose blood at an alarming rate. Miss Hague rushed out of the house and fetched help and Poole was taken to the Infirmary by Thomas Savage and Edward Wragg, where despite every effort to save him, he died shortly after his arrival. When she returned home from the Children's Hospital with her sick child, bearing some medicine, Mrs Poole was informed of her husband's suicide attempt. She found a note in her husband's handwriting bidding a last goodbye to his family and to all his friends. By the time Mrs Poole had reached the Infirmary, her husband was already dead.

Found with his Throat Cut in a Deepcar Garden

Mark had left two cards on the kitchen table with barely distinguishable notes written in pencil.

Tuesday 23 November. Thirty-two-year-old Mark Couldwell lived with his parents at Rock View, Carr Road, Deepcar. On Tuesday 22 November he went to bed earlier than usual, at 9.30pm. He got up about 5.45am the following morning, dressed, then went downstairs. His father heard him unbolt the back door and he called out to him. The reply he received startled him, as Mark shouted back, 'You'll never see me any more.' Mr Couldwell rushed downstairs but he found the back door had been locked. He then aroused his wife and other members of the family and they left the house through the front door and made a search for Mark in the still as yet dark, early morning. This hindered the search. On thinking that Mark might have gone to gone to his brother-in-laws house, Mr Couldwell went there and found his son lying in the garden with a dreadful gash in his throat, which ran from ear to ear, and a bloodstained razor close by. He was dead. At home Mark had left two cards on the kitchen table with barely distinguishable notes written in pencil.

An inquest was held before coroner Dossey Wightman, Esquire, at the *Royal Oak Hotel*, Deepcar on Friday 28 November. Mr Benjamin Couldwell, the deceased's father, was the only witness called. After stating that neither he, nor any members of his family knew of any reason why Mark should wish to take his own life, he said:

…My son was not in employment. He always enjoyed good health. Last Saturday he complained of feeling sick and was very quiet. He went to bed somewhat early on Tuesday night, and then appeared to be in his usual spirits.

The coroner said after reading the notes that there could be little doubt as to the state of the deceased's mind. Of what could be deciphered of the pencil notes, the first read:

Dear father and mother,

… Undecipherable … love to all

The second note read:

Dear mother,
I have gone forever. I don't … undecipherable … my father was
as bad as this. I do not bear it. Six hours off when ill. I shall not
see again. You can tell father to give my things to those of
… undecipherable … I am not sane, but obliged.

The jury returned a verdict of 'Suicide while in a state of
temporary insanity'.

Grinder's Suicide

… he was horrified to see his father-in-law leaning over the
kitchen sink with a deep gash across his throat and blood flowing
profusely from it.

Fifty-eight-year-old George Latham, a grinder, lived at 54
Sherrington Road, Highfield. He was on good terms with his
wife and relatives and had led a mostly trouble-free life. When
he was thirty-nine Mr Latham suffered a serious accident at
work, when a grindstone had broken and one of the
fragmented pieces had struck him on the head. He was
hospitalised for several weeks, during which time it had been
necessary to remove three pieces of bone from his skull. Since
then he had experienced periodic bouts of strange behaviour,
and although he was not a habitual drinker, whenever he
partook of alcohol, his condition was rendered what was
described by those who knew him as 'unimaginable'.

On Saturday 17 December, Latham over indulged himself
with strong drink but this did not result in any particularly
unusual occurrence. On Sunday however, he had only one
glass of beer and retired to bed at 10pm, apparently in good
spirits. At six o'clock the following morning, Monday 19
December, his wife got up and went to visit their married

daughter in Cecil Road, leaving her husband in bed. As she was leaving the bedroom he asked her what time it was. About half an hour later Mr Latham's son-in-law, Frederick John Fletcher, paid a visit to the house. He knocked on the door but received no reply. He opened the door, which was unlocked and entered the house. On going into the kitchen he was horrified to see his father-in-law leaning over the kitchen sink with a deep gash across his throat and blood flowing profusely from it. There was a bloodstained carving knife on the floor nearby. Mr Fletcher laid his father-in-law on the floor and went to fetch a surgeon, Mr Lockwood, but before he arrived Mr Latham was already dead. At the inquest at the *Royal Hotel*, Highfield, held on the evening of his death, the jury returned a verdict of 'suicide while suffering from temporary insanity'.

CHAPTER 7

The Woodhouse Murder

1893

… he could not bear to see Annie talking to another man. He said he would sooner kill her than see her do so and would think nothing of it.

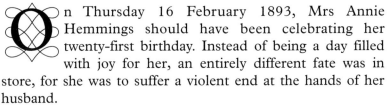n Thursday 16 February 1893, Mrs Annie Hemmings should have been celebrating her twenty-first birthday. Instead of being a day filled with joy for her, an entirely different fate was in store, for she was to suffer a violent end at the hands of her husband.

Born Annie Hague, she hailed from Normanton near Wakefield and had been married at All Saints' Church there, on 4 June the previous year. The marriage certificate described her husband, Edward Hemmings of 43 Benson Lane, as a collier and herself, Annie Hague as a spinster. Various accounts indicated that the couple were mismatched from the start. Annie had earned a reputation for hard work and honesty when, after leaving school, she took her first job as a general servant at the *Huntsman* public house. Good looking and gregarious by nature, she was regarded by some as a bit of a flirt. She was cheerful, light-hearted, chatty and high-spirited. She did, however, have a quick temper. She was also fond of pretty clothes. Despite having been brought up in a deeply religious household, Ted Hemmings was not without his faults. By temperament he was morose, sullen and melancholy. Those who knew him well described Hemmings as being moody and self-contained. He sometimes had to be asked a question five or six times before he would answer and he was apt to brood over fancied grievances and to nurse the spirit of revenge. Hemmings' feelings for his wife extended to manifest extreme jealousy within himself, whenever she became too friendly towards another man, even if that man should be a relative.

Up to the time he committed murder he had a clean record. His principal failing was that he was not an industrious man. Unbeknown to his soon-to-be wife, he shirked work whenever possible, resulting in him being short of money and, not long after their marriage, Annie was shocked to discover that her new husband was heavily in debt. Indeed in the months that followed, much of the furniture they acquired on hire purchase was repossessed due to Hemmings' inability to meet the instalment payments. Hemmings was so adverse to having to work for a living that he relied on others to knock him up, otherwise he simply didn't go.

Most likely in an attempt to escape creditors, Edward and Annie Hemmings moved from Normanton to Woodhouse on 20 August and lodged for a few weeks with Annie's sister, Anice Jones, at Canary Island, Woodhouse Mill. Once Hemmings had found work at Birley Colliery, they took lodgings in Robin Lane, Beighton buying furniture on hire purchase. Within two weeks the couple had quarrelled and Ted

A late-nineteenth century view of the Market Cross, Woodhouse. Old Barnsley

had walked out, leaving Annie to support herself by whatever means she could. Reduced to scraping a living by taking in her neighbour's washing, Annie was unable to pay the instalments and her new furniture was taken back to the department store from which it had only recently been purchased.

During this temporary absence from his wife Hemmings revealed to his sister-in-law, as he was subsequently to reveal to others, the depth of his jealousy. Indeed he confided to Anice Jones that he worshiped the ground his wife walked on. Ominously, he added that he could not bear to see Annie talking to another man. He said he would sooner kill her than see her do so and would think nothing of it. He produced a razor from his pocket with which he said he would cut Annie's throat and then his own. Annie told her sister that the quarrels stemmed from the fact that Ted was idle and would do nothing without being pushed along. By February 1893, Annie and Ted Hemmings had become reconciled and had moved into lodgings in Furnace Lane, Woodhouse, a house they shared with its owners, Mr and Mrs Kennington and three other lodgers. Mr Kennington was a shunter at Beighton Railway Station. This was to be the Hemmings' last marital home. Ted Hemmings, who was now working at Treeton Colliery, continued to visit his sister-in-law and to pour out his tale of woes. He told Mrs Jones that when they first moved into the Kennington's house their marital problems appeared to be at an end, but as time progressed Annie seemed to prefer spending time with the other lodgers than keeping him company. He said that she treated him like a dog.

At about 2.45am on the morning of Thursday 16 February 1893, one of the lodgers at the house in Furnace Lane, George Bradshaw, heard a woman's scream. He went to the landing and called out to see if all was well. Ted Hemmings replied to assure him that it was, so Mr Bradshaw went back to bed. At about four o'clock he heard someone leaving the house. He believed it was Ted Hemmings and was surprised at this as he habitually knocked Hemmings up at 4.30am each morning for work. Mr Bradshaw subsequently went downstairs and knocked on the Hemmings' door. When he got no reply he opened it and entered the room. He was faced with a blood-besmeared carpet and bed linen and immediately realised something was amiss. He summoned the other lodgers and instructed them to fetch the police. Mr Bradshaw then set off for work.

Police Constable Cole, who lived nearby, was the first to be informed. He sent for help. Sergeant Dempster was quickly at the scene. When a woman's blood-soaked body was discovered Dr Scott of Woodhouse was summoned. On examining the body Dr Scott was quick to confirm what the police officers already suspected: that the woman's wounds were not self-inflicted. Sergeant Dempster sent word to Sheffield and a short time before nine o'clock Superintendent Beilby arrived. He quickly took matters in hand and dispatched his officers out in search of Edward Hemmings.

Superintendent Beilby remained at the murder scene and after viewing the body, conducted a thorough examination of the room. He discovered a partially burned razor in the fire grate and the remains of some clogs. These clogs had been a bone of contention to Hemmings, who had shown them to his landlady the week before, after they had split, which had given him an excuse to return home early from work. He had told her that he was tired of life and did not care how soon it was ended. This led the police to suppose that Hemmings might commit suicide.

It was later ascertained that an axe was missing from the kitchen and it was believed that the axe and the razor already discovered were the murder weapons. The axe was discovered later in the day in a sump near Woodhouse Junction station. In the Hemmings' room were found carefully preserved books, which Ted Hemmings had gained as Sunday school prizes. Scripture text adorned the walls. Documents were discovered revealing that the Hemmings' had obtained furniture on hire from Mr Bailey of Rotherham and from Mr A H Banner of Attercliffe Road, Sheffield. There were also arrears owed on a sewing machine obtained from the Bradbury Machine Company, Wakefield. Another document showed that Hemmings was in arrears for a joint life insurance policy on himself and his wife with the Prudential Insurance Company. He owed them 4s. 2d., the amount being payable on the policy was £25 12s.

A description of the suspected murderer was released. Edward Hemmings stood approximately 5ft 6in tall. He was stoutly built, had black hair, a thick dark moustache and broad face. He was dressed in heavy moleskin trousers, black worsted jacket and vest and wore a light brown cap with peak front and a pair of old laced boots.

It was ascertained that Ted Hemmings had been seen leaving the house at 4.00am by a man named Hill, who was on his way to work. Mr Hill had followed him as far as Woodhouse Junction station. There were no reported sightings after that. There were speculations in various newspapers that Hemmings had committed suicide but this was not the case. On leaving Woodhouse Hemmings had headed for Doncaster. Arriving after dark he presented himself at the Guildhall, saying that he was a vagrant. They gave him a ticket, which procured him a bed in the workhouse. Next morning he walked to Featherstone, where he went to the house of someone he knew named Fox. The door was opened by the man's wife and she invited him in. Mrs Fox knew of the murder and expressed her surprise at seeing Hemmings alive and told him she though he would have drowned himself, to which Hemmings replied he thought too much about himself to do that. Mrs Fox made Hemmings a cup of tea and gave him something to eat. Afterwards he had a wash then set out for his parent's house. He had a change of heart as he got within a mile or so of their house and decided not to cause his mother any further grief. He headed for Normanton Police Station where he gave himself up. When he was searched he was found to be without means, his only possession being a miners' union card. Hemmings was curious to know if the hangman would get his clothes, a question he repeatedly asked the police officers. In the early hours of the following morning, Saturday 18 February, he was taken by train to Sheffield, where he arrived at 4.00am, from whence he was taken by foot to the West Riding Police Station in Burngreave Road.

Meanwhile, the inquest had been opened on Friday 17 February before coroner Dossey Wightman, esquire at the *Junction Hotel*, Woodhouse. Having taken evidence of identification of the dead woman, the coroner, before adjourning the proceedings until the following Wednesday, issued a burial certificate.

The *Sheffield and Rotherham Independent* reported on Tuesday 21 February:

> *... When it was known that the unfortunate young woman, in addition to being the victim of a brutal murder, was to be interred in a parish coffin and at the expense of the parish authorities, the people of Woodhouse were much exercised, and a public subscription was soon got up for the purpose of assisting the relatives to procure for the deceased what is so dear in the hearts of those in the humbler ranks of life – a 'decent burial'. While the parish found the coffin and paid for the grave the funds collected sufficed to put a little stain on the former* [an unadorned, unstained pine or deal parish coffin] *and to ornament it with metal handles and a breastplate. The body had remained in the room where the murder was committed in Furnace lane, and the coffin arrived about one o'clock yesterday, the appearance of which caused a small crowd to collect near. The body was then put into the coffin and the lid screwed down ... At three o'clock the cortege started from the house. No hearse or other vehicle was used the coffin being carried shoulder high to the cemetery, which is at least a mile and a half distant, and up hill most of the way. The bearers numbered twelve, and they carried the coffin in sets of four. Three policemen headed the procession, then came the coffin (which was not covered with a pall), and the bearers, with the mourners coming behind. None of the relatives of the husband were present.*

The inquest was resumed on Wednesday 22 February. George Bradshaw, a railway labourer, said that he lodged in Furnace Hill, Woodhouse, in a house owned by Charles Everitt Kennington and his wife, along with two other men and Ted and Annie Hemmings, who had occupied a room on the ground floor for about five weeks. He said he had last seen Mrs Hemmings alive at about 9.30pm the previous night when they were chatting in the kitchen, during which time Ted Hemmings was sitting alone in their room. The kitchen was used as a sort of living room by all the lodgers. Mr Bradshaw said his own room was immediately above the Hemmings'. He said at about 2.45am on the 15 February he heard what he described as a bit of a screech coming from the Hemmings' room. He got out of bed and shouted down the stairs:

Ted, Ted, what's amiss?

To which Hemmings replied:

Nowt.

Mr Bradshaw added that he knew that the noise had been made by Mrs Hemmings, because she had made the noise before when in fits. Mr Bradshaw then went back to bed.

The coroner: *You said something about fits. Do you know that the deceased woman was subject to fits?*

Bradshaw: *Yes.*

The coroner: *You have seen her in them?*

Bradshaw: *Yes, and have been with her at the time.*

The coroner: *Has she ever screamed in them?*

Bradshaw: *Yes.*

The coroner: *You say you thought she was in a fit?*

Bradshaw: *Yes, it is just what I did think, and nothing else.*

The coroner: *What did you hear next?*

Bradshaw: *I heard Hemmings go out about four o'clock.*

The coroner: *Was this his usual time for going out?*

Bradshaw: *No sir; I should think about half-past four reckoned to be his usual time.*

The coroner: *What did you see or hear then?*

Bradshaw: *I got up about five o'clock, and went down. I shook Hemmings' door and shouted.*

The coroner: *Did you get any reply?*

Bradshaw: *No; I heard nothing.*

The coroner: *What then?*

Bradshaw: *I knocked again at the door, and hearing nothing opened the door.*

The coroner: *What did you see?*

Bradshaw: *I saw blood on the clothes which were covered over her.*

The coroner: *Did you not see any body?*

Bradshaw: *No; I shouted, and the others came up.*

The coroner: *Before you did anything else?*

Bradshaw: *Yes.*

The coroner: *Who came?*

Bradshaw: *The two men who were lodging there Fred Ravendale and Benjamin Rowley. When they came I sent them for the police.*

The coroner: *Didn't you see the woman at all?*

Bradshaw: *No sir.*

The coroner: *Did you send for the police before you saw the woman at all?*

Bradshaw: *Yes.*

The coroner: *At that time you had not seen the deceased? The bed clothes were over her?*

Bradshaw: *Yes, she was covered from head to foot. I saw nothing at all of her; I only saw the blood. I believed she was there, but I could not see her.*

The coroner: *Did you see any more of it, or did you go away?*

Bradshaw: *I saw no more, and I went away to work.*

The coroner: *Had you heard any quarrel before then?*

Bradshaw: *No, not a word.*

The coroner: *Never before?*

Bradshaw: *No; at no time.*

The coroner: *You have never known Hemmings and his wife quarrel?*

Bradshaw: *No.*

The coroner: *Did you see any razors or knives?*

Bradshaw: *No sir; I saw nothing.*

Arthur William Scott, surgeon, practicing at Woodhouse, said he was called to the scene of the murder at half-past six in the morning. When he went to the house he was directed to a bedroom on the ground floor where he saw a woman's head and blood on the bedclothes; and also a large quantity of blood on the floor. He turned the bedclothes down and saw the body of the deceased. She was quite dead and appeared to have been in that condition for more than three hours. Rigor mortis had set in. Mr Scott said he found that the woman's throat had been cut from ear to ear, which probably caused the blood on the floor. There was also an incised wound above the left eye, which had fractured the skull and exposed the brain to view. He said that this wound had probably caused the blood on the bedclothes. Mr Scott was of the opinion that the wound on the head had been inflicted first and that it would cause the victim to have become insensible. He did not think it necessary to open the body, the cause of death clearly being the cut to the throat. The windpipe and gullet were completely divided and the spine laid bare. Mr Scott added that the wound gaped eight or ten inches and would have caused instant death. The victim might have lived a few hours after the blow to the head had the throat not been cut. He found the two middle fingers and the thumb on the left hand were nearly severed, the cuts being on the inside, as if Mrs Hemmings had seized a knife or sharp instrument and it had been drawn sharply out of her closed hand. There was also a cut on the right cheek and a small cut to another part of the neck. The body was lying with the head towards the fireplace and resting upon the left arm and was dressed only in night apparel. Mr Scott said he was in the room when a razor blade was found by Superintendent Beilby in the fireplace. He added that he had formed the opinion that the wound to the head had been caused by a hatchet, and the hatchet produced at the inquest was likely to have caused the injury. The blade exactly corresponded with the wound.

Other witnesses corroborated the events leading up to the murder at the end of which, in addressing the jury, the coroner said they had to say who in their opinion committed the murder. He then added:

The doctor said the wounds could not possibly have been self-inflicted. The question then arose, 'Who did it?' There could not be very much doubt about that if the evidence was worth anything at all. So far as I know there are no suspicions against any other person whomsoever with the exception of Edward Hemmings, her husband, who, it has been proved, had used threats that he would 'finish' her for some reason or other. She had been found 'finished.' Edward Hemmings absconded and this, of course, has always an ugly look. If anyone else had murdered the woman there would be no reason why he should have absconded…

The jury, after a few minutes deliberation, returned a verdict of 'wilful murder' against Edward Hemmings. Hemmings was committed to take his trial at the next assizes.

On Friday 24 February, Hemmings came up before West Riding magistrates, Alderman Michael Hunter and Mr T W Cadman, for a preliminary examination at Sheffield Town Hall. As the court was adjourning for lunch Annie Hemmings' eldest sister, Anice Jones, got up from her seat and went over to the prisoner. Before either the police or court officials could intervene the following exchange was heard to take place between them. Weeping bitterly, Anice said to her brother-in-law:

I am sorry it has come to this. If you had taken my advice it would not have happened. Speak the truth, Ted.

For the first time since his arrest Hemmings broke down and, holding out his hand to Anice, said:

Well, I confess I have done it.

At the close of the day's proceedings, when asked if he had anything to say, Hemmings said he had nothing to say and confirmed when asked that he wished to reserve his defence. The prisoner was then formally committed to take his trial at the next assizes commencing on 10 March.

Hemmings was tried at Leeds Assizes on Wednesday 15 March before Mr Justice Bruce. Mr Cyril Dodd QC, MP and Mr Arthur Bairstow prosecuted and Mr Walter Beverley defended. The trial opened at 10.30am and concluded at 6.00pm. The gallery was filled to capacity. Many spectators were men and woman who knew either the murdered woman or the prisoner and who had made their way to Leeds from Normanton. Hemmings had intended to conduct his own defence. However, some of his friends got together and raised the money to pay for the services of Bradford barrister Walter

Beverley, briefed by a solicitor from Wakefield, Edward Lodge. It seems that despite Hemmings having said he would go to the scaffold like a man, he was now determined to dodge that fatal journey if it could be avoided. On 16 March the *Sheffield And Rotherham Independent* reported that the defence had:

> *...got up as effective a defence as was possible under the circumstances. Immediately after the judge had taken his seat, Hemmings was placed in the dock. He walked with a firm, almost a defiant, step. His face was a little paler than on his last appearance in public, and, his hitherto clean shaven chin showed a growth of reddish beard. But his three weeks' detention at Wakefield had wrought no perceptible change in his demeanour. At no stage in the trial did he appear to be impressed with the gravity of his position, and but for the fact that he several times prompted his counsel or his solicitor – proving that he was intelligently following the evidence, and understood the advantage of making a point which would tell in his favour – a stranger might have supposed that he was merely an interested spectator in what was going on...As time went on the prisoner became somewhat fidgety, but not so much as might have been expected, having regard to the length of the trial.*

In his opening speech for the prosecution Mr Cyril Dodd said:

> *...it is my intention to lay before the jury a resume of the evidence in simple language and to endeavour to avoid any unnecessary comment. The prisoner was a collier, who, at the time of the death of his wife, was lodging with her at the house of a railway porter named Kennington, in Furnace Lane, Woodhouse, Sheffield. They had been lodging there for five weeks, and, so far as was known, got on comfortably there. They occupied one room on the ground floor of the house, and they were seen in this room about 9.30 o'clock on the night before the 16th February, by the landlady. The deceased was then preparing food for her husband to take with him to work the next day. The landlady [Mrs Eliza Kennington] said they seemed on very good terms at that time.*

Mr Dodd went on to outline George Bradshaw's version of events then went on to describe the scene of the murder:

... the dead body of the deceased was found lying on the floor of the bedroom, the skull being fractured, and the throat cut from ear to ear. The body was covered over with a sheet. There were cuts on the fingers of one of the deceased's hands, which indicated that she had struggled with her murderer. A large quantity of blood was found on the floor, on the stockings of the deceased, as if she had trodden in it, and on the clothes. Apparently she had been dealt a blow on the forehead with an axe, and her throat cut by a razor. A razor was found in the fire. An axe was missed from its usual place in the kitchen, and subsequently found in a gully a short distance away from Woodhouse. It appeared that after leaving the house the prisoner wandered to Normanton, where his friends lived, and where he was married, his wife having been in service there. He supposed under similar circumstances men did wander, mechanically, to places with which they had been familiar before. He went to the house of a Mrs [Charlotte] Fox, near Normanton, where he once lodged. Mrs Fox had heard of the murder and his supposed connection with it, and also broached the subject to him. He said he left his wife's body on the rug on the floor, and covered it with a cloth, and that he was wearing a cap that belonged to his wife, which he brought away because he wanted something belonging to her. He then said he loved the ground his wife trod on. Being asked why he had come back to Normanton, he replied that he wanted to see the old folks once again. Mrs Fox remarked that she would drown herself if she were in his position. In answer to that the prisoner said he had felt a weight upon his mind for several weeks, but now he felt as light as a feather. The next that was heard of the prisoner was that he gave himself up to Inspector Turton and Sergeant Ford at Normanton Police Station. He seemed to have had a conversation with the officers , to whom he admitted having killed his wife, but said he did not regret it, and announced his intention of going to the scaffold like a man. When he was handed over to Superintendent Beilby at Sheffield and charged with murder he said, 'Its right.' The evidence will show that the prisoner had carried about with him

a razor. I think the jury will have no difficulty in coming to the conclusion that the deceased was killed by the prisoner, and then comes the question – an important one but always a difficult one in such cases, to determine why he did it. What was the motive that actuated the prisoner in committing this crime? It is impossible to find for any crime of this gravity an adequate motive, at any rate which would operate upon the mind of a reasonable man and induce him to commit wilful murder ... The deceased woman seems to have had a strong desire to have a house of her own, and not to live in lodgings, while he [the prisoner] *seemed to have felt somewhat his inability to satisfy her by giving her a cottage such as she wanted. Some of the witnesses will show that the couple had changed their residence several times since they were married, while more than once they parted and came together again and lived fairly comfortably. It also appears from the evidence that the prisoner with or without reason was jealous, first of one lodger and then of another, so that their married life could not have been absolutely happy. There is evidence to show that the prisoner had talked of taking his wife's life some time before the crime was committed, and he showed a razor he had bought.*

In concluding his opening speech, Mr Dodd told the hushed courtroom:

The witnesses include several relatives of the deceased; and are mainly in a humble station in life. When the jury have heard their evidence I am sure that the jury will be convinced that they are people who have come into court with the intention of giving an accurate narrative of what they saw and knew. I submit that it will be impossible after the evidence has been heard, to doubt that the deceased has been the victim of a murder of a deliberate character, and that the prisoner is guilty of the crime.

The court heard much the same evidence as was given at the inquest and during committal proceedings.

Having heard all the evidence Mr Beverely addressed the jury on behalf of the prisoner:

I feel very keenly the weight of responsibility that rests upon me in defending this man. My responsibility however, is nothing compared to that of you, the jury, for according to what your verdict might be this unhappy man will either live or die. To kill is one thing, to commit murder is an entirely different kind of thing. That the prisoner killed his wife you can have no doubt but the question is did he kill her with malice of forethought? Did he premeditate the act? I invite you to bring in a verdict of manslaughter, an offence varying greatly in degree and one for which it is competent for his Lordship to commit to penal servitude for life. The prisoner has been shown to be of irreproachable character. He was well known in Normanton for some years, and all his acquaintances gave him a good name. Then he got married, and the marriage almost turned out to be his death warrant. A more ill-assorted union could not well have been entered into. He was of a jealous turn of mind, who loved his wife fondly, and would often coax her when he was in a temper. The wife was quick tempered and often defied her husband, telling him she should do just as she liked and take her own course. When the husband complained to Kelly [a male relative of whom Hemmings had become jealous] *of his conduct and that of the deceased, the latter never resented it, but told her husband it served him right. She had frequently said she did not care for him. I think you will not fail to infer from the evidence that the deceased was not quite the wife she ought to have been to the prisoner. Many circumstances have been mentioned to show that the prisoner was very fond of his wife. Even the night before the murder he was seen bending over his wife in an affectionate attitude, while she was knitting – spooning in fact* [indulging in demonstrative love making]. *That was not the conduct of a man who had a preconceived notion of destroying his wife's life. If he had premeditated such a crime he had plenty of opportunities of carrying it out during the time they lodged at the Kennington's. I ask you, gentlemen of the jury to believe that the prisoner was not serious when he uttered the threats. As to the razor, he was in the habit of using it, and it did not appear that he bought it for the purpose of murder. On the night before the murder the deceased was in the kitchen laughing and joking with the lodgers, while the prisoner was probably brooding over the old sore. I ask you to put yourselves in the place of this man, then perhaps you will be able to appreciate the amount of provocation the man felt. No doubt he had got into a frame of mind that made his susceptible to wrong motives, and one can understand how the lively spirit of his wife would be calculated to increase his anger. There was the occasion when the prisoner heard the deceased using severe language towards himself.*

It was at this point that Mr Justice Bruce interrupted the defence's closing speech to appraise the jury on a point of law, saying:

Gentlemen of the jury, I must impress upon you that no words, however opprobrious, could be considered in law provocation sufficient to reduce homicide to manslaughter, if the killing was effected by a deadly weapon.

Mr Beverley suggested that it might be otherwise in exceptional circumstances. To which his Lordship replied:

I am compelled to advise the jury according to the opinion I have expressed.

Mr Beverly made a final attempt to try to sway the jury in his client's favour by suggesting that Hemmings might have received greater provocation. He suggested that weapons might have been used by the deceased. He said there was no evidence to the contrary and there was no knowing what took place in the bedroom on that fatal morning.

The judge was once again prompted to interrupt the defence by pointing out:

Every homicide is deemed in law to be murder unless evidence is given to show it was otherwise.

Mr Beverley continued by contending that express malice had not been proved. He said there might have been a serious quarrel in the bedroom, and in the heat of the moment the prisoner might have snatched up the weapon which was nearest to hand and struck his wife. Mr Beverley concluded by saying:

All afternoon I have been endeavouring to save a drowning man, and I ask you, gentlemen of the jury, to assist me; and to supply any deficiency of which I might have been guilty in conducting this case on behalf of the prisoner.

His speech now over and the case for the defence being complete, the learned counsel resumed his seat. As he did so the courtroom erupted in spontaneous applause. It was now time for the judge to take over the proceedings. In his summing up Mr Justice Bruce told the jury:

…you have a serious and heavy duty to perform. You have to do justice to the prisoner and perform the duty imposed upon you by the State to give a verdict according to the evidence. If you are satisfied that according to the evidence, the prisoner is guilty of wilful murder, I am sure however painful that duty might be, you will bring in a verdict of guilty. A good deal has been said by the learned counsel who so ably defended the prisoner about the absence of evidence of express malice. But in law every man has to take the consequences of his own acts. When a man strikes his wife or any other person on the head with a deadly weapon, from the very act itself there is, in the eye of the law, malice. The law implied malice to a man who shoots at another man with a pistol, or stabs at him with a knife. It is not for you to seek evidence of expressed malice. You have to consider whether what was done was done under such circumstances of provocation it would justify the act. If a man killed another in self-defence it was no crime; if done under great provocation the act was not justifiable, but the crime might be reduced to the minor one of manslaughter. It is highly improbable that this woman's death was caused by a person in a momentary fit of passion caused by provocation. Even if there were provocation by words – and that was not proved – mere words of reproach, however grievous, is not sufficient provocation to reduce homicide to manslaughter, if effected by deadly weapons. In the present case there was not merely the blow on the head, but the terrible gash on the throat. The poor woman did not die with but one mark upon her body.

I do not think all this could have been done in a momentary passion produced by provocation of words. The prisoner, in his numerous conversations, has not said his wife provoked him. He never made any suggestion that his wife made an attack upon him. The only suggestion was as to certain words she had used about him in Mrs Kennington's kitchen, and that took place some considerable time before the prisoner killed her. You can have no doubt how the deceased came by her death and who killed her, and there is no evidence of sufficient provocation to reduce the crime to manslaughter. It is my duty to tell you that the words the deceased woman had used are not sufficient for that purpose.

The jury, having listened to the judge's summing up, retired. After discussing the evidence they returned after thirty-five minutes and delivered their verdict. They found that the prisoner was 'guilty of the wilful murder of his wife' but they recommended him to mercy. The Clerk of Arraigns then rose and asked if the prisoner had anything to say about why sentence of death should not be passed, to which Hemmings replied that he would like to make a few remarks. He then launched into a long a rambling speech in which he cited incidents pertaining to his jealousy concerning his wife's association with various male relatives and friends. The speech made little sense to the spectators and at one point Hemmings broke down before continuing. He paused for breath and the judge, clearly thinking Hemmings had finished, began to pronounce sentence, at which point Hemmings attempted to continue with his speech. On being told he could not do so by an official, he acquiesced, although it was clear he still had more to say.

Mr Justice Bruce then addressed the prisoner in the dock:

After a most careful trial, and after listening with attention to the most able defence delivered by your counsel, the jury have found you guilty of the crime of murder. They have also recommended you to mercy, and in reference to that all I can say is that it shall be forwarded to the proper quarter. The evidence given in the court today proves that you have been guilty of a most cruel and brutal murder. You have with heartless violence taken the life of a woman whom you were bound by every obligation to succour and protect. You sent her without warning to eternity. You will have an opportunity of preparation which you denied her. Let me implore you eagerly to embrace the opportunities of spiritual consolation which will be offered to you in prison.

The judge then pronounced sentence of death on the prisoner.

The jury's recommendation for mercy was ignored. Various newspapers, including the *Sheffield And Rotherham Independent* reported on Saturday 1 April that Hemmings' solicitor Mr Edward Lodge had received news from the Home Secretary, Mr Asquith, that he would not accede to the petition for a reprieve and that the law must take its course. On Monday 3 April, Hemmings was visited in the condemned cell at Armley Gaol, Leeds, by his parents Emmanuel, and Sarah Hemmings, his brother Thomas, his sister Sarah and his brother-in-law John Baker. They remained with him for twenty minutes. Hemming's seventy-three-year-old father left Armley with his family, from the look on his face it was evident that the thought of his son's fate had told upon him considerably. Later in the day James Billington the executioner, arrived at Armley from Bolton, for his overnight stay. The following morning at

Armley Gaol, Leeds.
John D Murray collection

8.00am Edward Hemmings was hanged in the permanent execution shed adjoining the cookhouse. Billington gave him a drop of 7ft 5in. Death was instantaneous. Forty seconds after the clock had struck eight the black flag was hoisted.

On Thursday 6 April a letter was published in the *Sheffield And Rotherham Independent*. It was written by Edward Hemmings in the condemned cell at Armley Gaol and sent to Thomas Cressy of Normanton Common. Part of the letter is transcribed here:

If ever there was a man tried to do what was right and tried all as ever he knew how to live a Christian's life, I tried to live one, but, alas! there came a time when I was doing no work. I was living with Mrs Fox, but we flitted with them and went to Sourbrigg, Featherstone Common, they call it. Well, what with doing no work, and running into debt at my lodgings, I seemed to grow colder and colder, and to stop away from meeting[s], and at last I stopped going altogether. One day I stood against Birch's grocer's shop, and a young man came by – an old companion –and begged of me to go and have a drink, and doing no work, and running my board money on, and to tell you the truth I seemed miserable. What with one thing and what with another I yielded, and I am sorry to say I stopped and got drunk … I have a favour to ask. The first Sunday night after you get this can you arrange that you take to your text 'What shall it profit man though he gain the whole world and lose his own soul,' or 'What would a man give in exchange for his soul.' I forget which chapter but I dare say you will know where to look for it … When I committed the murder, even a minute or two after it was done, I would freely have given ten thousand worlds if but then in my possession. But it was too late. The truth was not spoken at the trial, and I shall be able to prove it when we come to stand before the judgement bar of God. I am pleased to know this – that when we appear before our Maker to give an account of the deeds done in this body, thank God the truth will have to be told up there …

From
Edward Hemmings
Armley Gaol

CHAPTER 8

The Walkley Murder

1923

He let me in by the back door. As he was locking the door, I hit him on the head with the hatchet. He fell to the floor, and then I hit him twice more.

For most of his working life John William Eastwood earned his living as a chimney sweep. He married Ethel Gill in 1902. She ran her own buffing workshop in Sheffield and they had three children together, two of whom, like their parents, were christened John William and Ethel. Arnold, the second of the Eastwood's children, had died at the age of three in 1910. At the time of their father's arrest for wilful murder on 29 July 1923, John and Ethel were aged twenty and fourteen respectively. John (or Jack, as he was known by some) Eastwood had managed to evade service in the armed forces during the Great War, having been rejected by the army because he suffered from neurasthenia (a psychological disorder characterized by chronic fatigue and weakness). He did not work after 1915 and was, for some time, a patient at the Royal Infirmary. He was also treated for syphilis at Eccleshall Asylum in February 1915. The cumulative effects of these afflictions had given him the excuse to hang up his chimney sweep's brushes. Meanwhile Ethel continued to run her buffing workshop very successfully. About eighteen months before the murder took place the Eastwoods had diversified and John had become the licensee of the *Bay Horse Inn*, situated at 72 Daniel Hill Street, Walkley, at its junction with Harworth Street, where they now lived. During his relatively short time as a publican he had developed a relationship with one of his customers, a young married woman named Mildred Parramore. He was then aged thirty-nine, she, twenty-two. Such was his infatuation with Mildred that they decided to run off together. They did so on 30 June 1923.

What seemed like a good idea clearly turned out otherwise and by 12 July John and Mildred were both back in Sheffield. Mildred's husband was happy to have her back but Ethel refused her husband not only her bed but also her roof. From that point onwards Eastwood, having relinquished the running of the *Bay Horse Inn* to the care of Ethel when he left her for a younger woman, she now refused to even speak to him. Eastwood was left with no choice but to find a bed wherever he could.

One of the casual staff at the inn was forty-eight-year-old John Joseph Clark, who helped out as barman and potman. He worked in the cutlery industry as a spoon and fork stamper but he was also experienced in the licensing trade, having onetime been steward with his wife, Eva, stewardess of the Institute of the Antediluvian Order of Buffaloes, in West Street. John Clark was himself an enthusiastic Buffalo. He had helped out at the *Bay Horse Inn* for a long time. He and Ethel lived with their two sons, Jack, aged eighteen and Harry, aged ten, and Clark's seventy-four-year-old father, in Lister Road. Eastwood and Clark got on well together and Eastwood asked Clark to put in a good word with Ethel for him, in the hope that she would take him back. When Clark's pleas on Eastwood's behalf did not work, Eastwood made something of a nuisance of himself by turning up in the evenings at the inn for a drink. He had been sleeping at various addresses since his return from Liverpool, including the home of Mr and Mrs Arthur Hilton at No 1 Court, 8 House, Greaves Street, from which address he had been scraping a living by resuming his old trade as a chimney sweep. Eastwood had also slept on the couch at the home of John and Eva Clark at 20 Lister Road. On several occasions he had refused to leave the inn at the end of his drinking session and it had been necessary for Ethel to call the police to persuade him to leave. During his absence in Liverpool, Ethel had applied to have the license of the *Bay Horse Inn* transferred to herself, which was ratified by the magistrates at the transfer sessions on Wednesday 26 July.

When John Eastwood went to the inn that evening, he was confronted by the name Ethel Eastwood painted above the doorway, displaying to all that his tenure as licensee was over and he was now officially an ex-publican.

Although John Clark and his wife were very happily married, Eastwood had somehow got it into his head that during his absence in Liverpool Clark and his own wife, Ethel, had forged an attachment. As far as anyone could tell there was nothing amiss between Eastwood and Clark, indeed as the *Sheffield And Rotherham Daily Independent* reported on Monday 30 July:

> *Eastwood and Clark met continuously, and were quite amiable to each other, and they chatted together at Saturday dinner-time. On Saturday night Mrs. Eastwood stated her husband came to the inn, and he was quite sober, one of his drinks being a 'lemon dash'. He asked to stay the night, and when this was refused he showed a strong disinclination to leave at closing time. Eventually he left reluctantly, after quite peaceful persuasion …*

At 1.30am on Sunday morning, John and Eva Clark were asleep in bed at their home in Lister Road. Mrs Clark was wakened by someone throwing pebbles at the window. She looked out and saw it was Eastwood. Thinking he wanted somewhere to sleep for the night she roused her husband, who got up and went downstairs. Shortly afterwards she heard the door bang and sounds of a scuffle taking place. She went downstairs and found her husband just inside the kitchen by the mangle, rolling about on the floor with blood streaming from his head and Eastwood standing over him with a hatchet in his hand. Eastwood took to his heels without uttering a word, as the Clark's son, Jack, came downstairs and helped his mother carry his badly wounded father into the kitchen.

Eastwood immediately went from the Clark's house in Lister Road to Burgoyne Road Police Station, where he gave himself up. He said to Inspector Hughes:

> *I want you to go to 20 Lister Road – I believe I have done Jack Clark in with a hatchet, which I have thrown away, probably in the chapel yard in Walkley Road.*

On Monday 30 July, the same day that Eastwood made his first appearance before Sheffield magistrates, the *Sheffield And Rotherham Independent*, in their report of the murder under the headline **BARMAN ATTACKED WITH A HATCHET**, published an interview with Clark's eighteen-year-old son, Jack. He told the reporters:

BARMAN ATTACKED WITH A HATCHET.

FOUND DYING AT KITCHEN DOOR.

Early Morning Crime in Sheffield.

SENSATIONAL SEQUEL.

Ex-Publican Detained at Police Station.

A terrible tragedy occurred in a quiet street in the Walkley district of Sheffield early yesterday morning. John Clark (48), stamper, of 20, Lister road, was found by his wife and son about 1.30 a.m. lying across the open arway of the kitchen of his house, a pool of blood, with several severe in his head.

ied at the Royal Infirmary at n. following an operation. minutes after the tragic dis-y a man gave himself up to the e at Burgoyne road Police ion and made a statement, as a it of which he was detained, and appear before the Sheffield strates to-day.

man in custody is John William wood (37), a chimney sweep and censer of the Bay Horse Inn, ield Hill street, where Clark was doyed as potman and bar tender road and Clark were on terms of ndship and had, in fact, spoken each other amicably only a few urs before Clark's death.

HORRIFIED FAMILY.

graphic story of the attack on his was told to a representative of "The ld Independent" by Mr. Jack Clark, year-old son of the victim of the

annily, comprising Mr. and Mrs. he two sons, Jack and Harry and their grandfather, an old h were in bed when Clark was I hea knocking on the back door. ard father go downstairs, and ard sother six bangs, and I it of bed and ran downstairs. also ran downstairs, and at the bottom of the stairs x lying in the doorway, a heap against the mangle with blood all round him, red on the wall. He had d in his head, on round the hand.

junction of Daniel Hill street and Har-worth street, 18 months ago, Mr. Eastwood being the licensee.

The victim of the present tragedy was employed casually and for long spells, as barman at the inn, and his relations with both parties were most cordial and satisfactory.

Mr. and Mrs. Eastwood parted some little time ago, and Mrs. Eastwood refused admittance to her husband when he came back.

Following the estrangement the licence for the hotel was transferred to Mrs. Eastwood, the Sheffield justices assenting to the transfer duly last Wednesday.

Since that time the husband has been to the Bay Horse many times as a customer, but his wife did not speak to him. On one or two occasions Eastwood is stated to have refused to leave the building at closing time, and the police were called to "persuade" him.

Friendly with Clark.

During all this time Eastwood and Cl met continuously, and were quite amiable to each other, and they chatted together at Saturday dinner-time.

On Saturday night Mrs. Eastwood stated her husband came to the inn, and he was quite sober, one of his drinks being a "lemon dash." He asked to

John Clark, the victim.

slay the night, and when this was refused he showed a strong disinclination t leave at closing time.

Eventually he left, reluctantly, afte quite peaceful persuasion.

Mrs. Eastwood said she had a daughter Ethel, aged 20, and a son, John William aged 14.

Her husband, she said, was subject to increase fits. His father and uncle died in an asylum.

HATCHET FOUND.

MISSED FROM BACKYARD OF THE INN.

Mrs. Eastwood paid a glowing tribute t the character of the victim of the traged who had tried to effect a rec his husband and wife.

A cutting from the Sheffield and Rotherham Independent, *Monday 30 July 1923, giving details of the event in Lister Road in the early hours of the previous day, with a picture of the murder victim – John Clark.*
Sheffield & Rotherham Independent

I heard father go downstairs, and then I heard about six bangs, and I sprang out of bed and ran downstairs. My mother also ran downstairs, and I found her at the bottom of the stairs. Father was lying in the doorway huddled up in a heap against the mangle in the kitchen, with blood all round him, and blood spattered on the wall. He had some awful wounds on his head. Mother saw a man run round the passage with an axe in his hand. Father mumbled something as we carried him into the kitchen, and I ran to fetch Dr Exell, and found a police officer present on my return. They took father to the Royal Infirmary in the Fire Brigade ambulance, and he died soon after.

Newspapers also mentioned Mrs Ethel Eastwood's comments, when she was visited by reporters at the *Bay Horse Inn*, during Sunday. One report said a touching feature was Mrs Eastwood's deep concern for the dependents of her late employee. As she burst into tears she said:

I am thinking of his wife and children, their breadwinner is gone.

Reports went on to say the Mrs Eastwood had also announced her intention of visiting Mrs Clark. Throughout Sunday the inn remained opened and the bar was filled with customers discussing the terrible events of just a few hours before. The events had caused a sensation on the streets of Walkley and Hillsborough, where Eastwood and Clark were well known.

On the same day as the wider public of Sheffield were reading in the newspapers about the events in Walkley, in the early hours of the previous day, John William Eastwood was making his first appearance at Sheffield Police Court before magistrates Mr J C Clegg and Mr R G Blake, charged with the wilful murder of John Joseph Clark. On the following day the *Sheffield Daily Telegraph* reported that:

... he maintained a cool and collected bearing. A heavily-built man, with bronzed and stern features, he was dressed in a blue suit, but was minus collar or tie. A hatchet which it is said will play an important part in the case, was exhibited in court...

During the proceedings Inspector Hughes said:

> *...I ordered him* [Eastwood] *to be detained while I made enquiries...On arriving at the house I found the back door closed, and the lights full on. I pushed at the door and it opened just a few inches. I then saw the naked foot of a man. I pushed the door forward and was able to get inside. There I found the unconscious body of a man who was lying full-length on his back with his feet towards the door. The man was only wearing trousers and a shirt. I examined the man and discovered two wounds on the back of his head. One was a very deep wound. Inside the house I saw the injured man's wife standing on the stairs. She said to me 'Jack Eastwood has done that; I don't know what he has done it for.' I sent for the ambulance and just afterwards the doctor arrived. A son of 18 years had slipped away for him. In the meantime I had rendered first aid. Then the man was taken to the Royal Infirmary, where it was seen that he was too unconscious to allow for a deposition being taken. A consultation of the doctors was held and Clark was operated upon. At about 8.45am the same morning the injured man passed away. At 10.30am yesterday morning, after cautioning the prisoner, I charged him with the wilful murder of Clark. He replied, 'Yes, sir.' On examining a chapel yard at the junction of Walkley Bank Road and Walkley Road, I discovered on the footpath about 500 or 600 yards from the deceased's man's home, the axe* [produced in court]. *There was fresh blood on it. I afterwards visited the* Bay Horse Hotel *in Daniel Hill Street, where the accused had been licensee up to a month ago, leaving on account of domestic trouble. The axe was identified as their property, and it was in the yard on Saturday evening.*

Members of the public who had filled the courtroom to capacity were disappointed if they hoped to hear a dramatic story concerning any further details of the crime. The evidence given was very formal and on application of the police Eastwood was remanded until the following Saturday. An inquest was held on Tuesday 31 July at the Coroner's Court in Nursery Street, before J Kenyon Parker, Esquire.

The first witness was Eva Clark. She described how Eastwood had come to the house and what had occurred immediately after her husband had gone downstairs. The next witness to be called was Arthur John Hilton, who lived in Greaves Street. He said that Eastwood had been sleeping at his house for nearly a fortnight, 'in consequence of trouble at home'. Early on Sunday morning Eastwood called at Mr Hilton's house when he and his wife were in bed. He let himself in with a latch key and entered their bedroom. Mr Hilton said that Eastwood was sober, then added:

> *I noticed the head and shaft of an axe in his trouser pocket, this struck me as unusual ... Eastwood said to me, 'I am going to knock him up.' He then chucked the key on the dressing table, saying, 'I shall not require it any more ... Before he left the house I said to him, 'Don't be a fool.'*

Dr E E Clayton of the Royal Infirmary, who had conducted the post mortem examination on Clark's body, provided the medical evidence evidence. He said:

> *Clark was admitted suffering from three wounds in the back of the head, two probably caused by the blunt side of some instrument. A gap had been caused in the skull that was six inches long, and two-and-a-half inches wide, and the cause of death was the fracture.*

The next witness called was twenty-two-year-old Mildred Parramore. She was very emotional as she gave her evidence and said that she had known Eastwood for several months and that she had a conversation with him on the morning of Saturday 28 July, after she had bumped into him in Wallace Road, during the course of which Eastwood had said:

> *If Ethel doesn't have me back, I'm going to do him in.*

Although Eastwood had not referred to John Clark by name, Mrs Parramore said she believed that was who he was talking about as he had said that kind of thing before.

Inspector Hughes was called next and repeated the evidence he had given at the Police Court the previous day. The last witness called was Constable Peach who said following Eastwood's arrest, when he was taking him to the cells, he had told him:

He let me in by the back door. As he was locking the door, I hit him on the head with the hatchet. He fell to the floor, and then I hit him twice more.

In his summing up, the coroner, in making reference to the police witnesses, pointed out that there was little doubt about the strict admissibility of certain statements, because they were made by a police officer who had not cautioned the prisoner making them. However, he added that he had admitted them, as they could not be ignored, being in the nature of a voluntary admission, and not being extorted by any examination or questioning. He also pointed out to the jury that the question of sanity or insanity of the prisoner was not a matter for them to decide. The jury returned a verdict of 'wilful murder,' which was received by Eastwood with his head bowed. As the coroner committed the prisoner to take his trial at Leeds Assizes, Eastwood was visibly shaking and his hands twitched uncontrollably. At the end of the proceedings, Eastwood was taken back to the Central Police Station.

On Friday 3 August, a large crowd had gathered outside the deceased's man's house in Lister Road to watch the funeral cortege leave for St Mary's church, where a similar sized crowd had also gathered. Ethel Eastwood was one of the mourners. Following a short service John Clark's body was conveyed to the parochial cemetery nearby, where he was buried in the lower part of the cemetery. His wife, Eva, did not join him there until 1957. The grave they share is unmarked.

On the following Saturday Eastwood made a brief appearance at Sheffield Police Court before Mr C Whitehead and Mr W Bush, when Detective Inspector Elliott asked that he be remanded until the following Friday. The remand was granted. After several further adjournments, Eastwood's committal proceedings were resumed on 21 August, when

Mr J E Wing appeared for the prosecution and Eastwood was represented by the Sheffield solicitor Charles Wyril Nixon, who quickly showed that the basis of the defence was grounded in establishing Eastwood's insanity.

Under cross-examination Eva Clark was questioned about the relationship between Eastwood and her husband. She said that relations had been good and she knew of no reason why Eastwood would wish to hurt her husband. Inspector Hughes was asked information concerning Eastwood's background and family history, to which he replied:

My enquiries show that he was admitted to the Eccleshall institution in February 1915 suffering from syphilis. His father and uncle both died in Wadsley asylum, the former from paralysis, the latter from melancholia following war service.

Dr Brockham of the Royal Infirmary, one of the doctors who had treated Clark, gave evidence about his injuries. Then, with reference to Eastwoods he was also asked about the link between syphilis, insanity and suicide. The packed courtroom heard Dr Brockham say:

Many people with a history such as Eastwood had were mentally normal. Syphilis would not predispose a sufferer to suicide until he was quite off his head and if a man so suffering did go insane he did not recover.

William Weeks, who was walking out with Eastwood's daughter, said that not long after his return from Liverpool, Eastwood had, on 15 July, shown him a razor, and as he did so, said to him:

This is for Jack Clark. He has told me to find somewhere else to sleep today. His wife objects to me sleeping on their couch and it means I shall be homeless. That's after promising me shelter.

Weeks went on to say when Eastwood brandished the razor again later in the day and reiterated his threat, he had taken it off him. He said during the fourteen months he had known him, Eastwood's conduct had always been queer. He had heard him threaten Mrs Eastwood on several occasions and he was always talking about doing the whole lot of them in. Such were Mrs Eastwood's concerns that her husband would harm someone that she had asked him to go and live at the *Bay Horse Inn* with them.

When Mildred Parramore was called she answered some of the questions put to her with no small degree of embarrassment, as unlike at the inquest, when the questions asked only served to determine how Clark had met his death, more probing questions about the background to the case obliged Mildred to reveal the facts of her infidelity. During the course of questioning, Mildred said that while they were in Liverpool Eastwood had talked of killing himself. The remainder of the prosecutions case was based on evidence already heard at the inquest. After all witnesses had been called, when asked if he had anything to say, Eastwood replied that he wished to reserve his defence. The magistrates duly committed him for trial.

Eastwood's trial took place at the West Riding Assizes and was held on Friday 7 December at Leeds Town Hall, before Mr Justice Talbot. Mr W J Waugh KC and Mr W Hedley appeared for the Crown, Mr F J O Coddington, for the defence. The trial lasted all day. In his opening speech Mr Waugh said:

I submit that this is a most deliberate, premeditated murder, that the prisoner knew what he had done, and that he gave himself up for that reason. The facts of the case are sordid, and there can be no doubt that the motive of the murder was jealousy. The prisoner was for a time licensee of the Bay Horse [Inn], *and Clark had acted at nights as a barman. On the evidence to be given and on statements of the prisoner himself, there can be no doubt that Clark and the prisoner's wife were upon intimate terms. The prisoner left his wife on June 30th, and went away with a married woman name Parramore, for several days; then returned to Sheffield and quarrelled with his wife; next, for some days before Clark's death, the accused lodged with a man named Hilton in Greaves Street, Hillsborough. On the night of July 28th*

> *Eastwood went into the bedroom where Hilton and his wife were sleeping, with an axe in his trousers pocket, and said: 'I'm going to knock him up.' He also threw his keys on the table and said: 'I shan't want them any more.'*

Before Mr Waugh could continue one of the jurymen was taken ill and collapsed in the box. Proceedings had to be halted while a replacement juror, who also happened to be a man, was sworn in. On resuming his speech, Mr Waugh said:

> *Clark went from Hilton's to Lister Road, and Mrs Clark heard something rattling on a window and saw Eastwood outside. Her husband went downstairs to open the door, and just afterwards she heard a noise. Going downstairs, she saw her husband reeling in the doorway, and Eastwood running away with a hatchet. Her husband was in a terrible condition, having three wounds on his head … When the murdered man was examined by doctors it was found his case was hopeless …*

When Dr E E Clayton was called to give evidence there was no answer. Then his Lordship was told the doctor had sailed for China since the magisterial proceedings, and he was prompted to remark:

> *It is extremely wrong to interfere with the course of justice in this way.*

The judge then imposed a fine of £50 on Dr Clayton, in his absence.

During the proceedings a large crowd had gathered outside the Town Hall to listen to the results of the city's candidates in the General Election. Spasmodic bouts of loud cheering broke out as the results were announced, which contrasted widely with the events within the courtroom.

Police Constable Beresford said he received a complaint at the Police Station from Eastwood about Clark's attention to his wife. Eastwood said to the constable:

It's a bit of a bugger if a man can't do as he likes in his own house. This man can come in when he likes, and if I can't, I will kill him.

Police Constable Ellis said that he heard Eastwood say outside the Police Station:

It's all over Clark and my wife. If I can't have her, Clark won't. I will kill him.

In addition to the witnesses already heard at the inquest and the Police Court proceedings, the Crown called Dr R D Worsley, medical officer at Armley Gaol, and his assistant Dr Hoyland Smith. Dr Worsley said in his opinion Eastwood was a sane man. During his period of observation he had seen nothing whatever to indicate that his mind was unhinged. While other medical evidence was being given concerning the state of the prisoner's health, Eastwood became extremely agitated and was clutching at his throat. Mr Coddington said that his client was feeling unwell. Eastwood was removed from the courtroom and when he returned after a few minutes had elapsed he looked much better. Sheffield Police Surgeon, Dr G Carter, gave evidence concerning Eastwood's state of mind. During his evidence he remarked:

I do not believe that more than one third of the people who commit suicide are insane ...

As the medical evidence continued the defence bided their time until an opportunity arose for them to attempt to influence the jury as to the state of mind of the prisoner. When it did, Mr Coddington interjected on the prisoner's behalf, submitting that he was insane at the time of the crime. Mr Coddington's interjection was fortuitous, because when Dr Hoyland Smith, assistant medical officer at Armley Gaol, was called, his evidence appeared to add weight to the defences claim regarding the prisoner's sanity. Contrary to what his colleague Dr Worsley had said regarding the prisoner's state of mind, Dr Hoyland Smith expressed the opinion that he considered Eastwood was not conscious of the gravity of the act he committed, but he probably realised an hour afterwards what he had done. During cross-examination of the medical witnesses, the defence had managed to include all the evidence at their disposal to highlight Eastwood's background concerning insanity in his family, as well as his own afflictions. In his closing speech Mr Coddington reiterated that his client was insane at the time he committed the crime, and stated that the accusation of misconduct against the wife was not proved. He invited the jury to return a verdict of 'guilty but insane'.

During his Lordship's summing up Eastwood became very restless and it was not long before he was taken ill again. His Lordship was able to continue with his summing up and the jury retired, giving Eastwood sufficient time to compose himself. They returned a little under three-quarters-of an hour later to a hushed courtroom. Eastwood leaned on the dock rail to support himself, as the foreman delivered the jury's verdict. They found the prisoner 'guilty, with a recommendation to mercy'. As soon as the verdict was announced Eastwood collapsed in the dock and had to be assisted to his feet.

When the Clerk of Arraigns asked if the prisoner had anything to say why sentence should not be passed, Eastwood replied:

Whatever happened I never meant to do it.

After telling Eastwood that he had been convicted on evidence that had left the jury with no alternative but to bring in a verdict of guilty. Having donned the black cap, Mr Justice Talbot continued:

You must not count upon the sentence not being executed, and I do earnestly beseech that you will use the short time which is yours to seek mercy where it only can be found.

His Lordship then passed sentence of death upon the prisoner, following which Eastwood had to be carried from the dock in a state of collapse.

Eastwood's lawyers did not appeal against the conviction. A petition was organised in the hope of securing a reprieve. It contained over 10,000 signatures. The date of Eastwood's execution was scheduled to take place at Armley Gaol on Friday 28 December. On the day before the scheduled execution the Home Secretary announced that he could not grant Eastwood a reprieve and the law must take its course.

On Thursday night Eastwood was transferred from the condemned cell to a smaller cell nearer the scaffold. Although he passed what officials described as a 'fair night', when the time came on Friday morning to walk the few steps across the yard to the execution shed, it was necessary to assist him. In addition to the warders and prison doctor, those in attendance at the execution were the Sheriff of the County Colonel F R T Gascoigne, the Governor of Armley Gaol Captain A C Scott, the acting Under-Sheriff B Dodsworth, Esquire, and the Chaplain. The executioner was John Ellis.

At the inquest held later that morning before Leeds City Coroner, W H Clarke, Esquire, a verdict was returned that death was due to dislocation of the vertebrae caused by hanging of the neck, and properly carried out in accordance with sentence of death passed. Eastwood's body was subsequently buried within the precincts of Armley Gaol.

On Saturday 29 December the *Sheffield And Rotherham Independent* reported:

Mr G. W. Gill, of 100 West-street, Sheffield, who organised the petition asking for a reprieve of Eastwood, visited the condemned man in his cell at Armley Gaol, Leeds, on Monday. To a representative of the Sheffield and Rotherham Independent, *yesterday, Mr Gill said that Eastwood 'kept up his pecker like a man.' ... 'He ate well and slept well, and said that he was happy to go. He was ready to die. He would be better dead than living under the conditions he had been for the last few months.' ... 'I could tell a lot,' said Mr Gill, 'but at present I cannot. Eastwood told me all about it, and who was behind it all; but I cannot say anything about that now ... 'He realised he had to die, and said that the sooner the end came the better ...' Eastwood wished to thank everybody who signed the petition. He had no regrets, except that he was sorry for Mrs Clark, the widow of the victim.*

The case of John Eastwood has two distinctions. This was the first capital case to be tried by Mr Justice Talbot (Sir George John Talbot [1861–1938]), who had only been appointed a judge earlier that year. John Eastwood was also the last person to be hanged by John Ellis (1874–1932), who hanged some high profile murderers during the early twentieth century, including Doctor Crippen, Frederick Seddon and George Joseph Smith (the 'Brides in the Bath' murderer). Ellis resigned in 1924. In the course of twenty-three years he had executed 203 men and women. Later that year Ellis tried to commit suicide. After drinking brandy heavily, he attempted to shoot himself through the head. He appeared before a magistrate who told him, 'I'm sorry to see you here Ellis. I have known you for a long time. If your aim was as true as some of the drops you have given, it would have been a bad job for you.' He was bound over to keep the peace for a year and to stay away from strong drink and thoughts of suicide. Ellis became very depressed in the years that followed. His health was not good and he continued to drink heavily. In September 1932, nine years after he had first attempted suicide, he slit his throat with a cut-throat razor. This time he did not bungle it. The coroner's verdict was 'suicide while of unsound mind'.

Sources and Further Reading

Chapter One: Meting Out of Justice In Sheffield
Sheffield And Rotherham Independent, Thursday September 15 1892
Sheffield Daily Telegraph, January 2, April 8 1905, January 16 1914
A Handbook on Hanging, Charles Duff, Putnam, London, 1928. Revised and enlarged edition,1961
The Sheffield Hanged, David Bentley, ALD Design & Print, Sheffield, 2002
The Sheffield Murders 1865–1965, David Bentley, ALD Design & Print, Sheffield, 2003
A History of Sheffield, David Hey, Carnegie Publishing, Lancaster, 1998
Illustrated Police News, August 7 1880

Chapter Two: Foul Deeds from 1766–1923
Sheffield Iris, July 19, August 2 1793, December 17 1799
Sheffield Mercury, April 5, 29, May 3 1834
The Times, August 21, 1793, March 20, 21 1800, December 21 1923
Sheffield Daily Telegraph, May 30 1881, January 15 1892, September 23, December 2 1922, January 5, 6, July 14 1923
Sheffield And Rotherham Independent, February 1, March 29 1834, March 17 1860, November 18, December 26 1868, November 1, December 19 1868, February 2 1869, March 11, 26, 29 1869, August 7 1872, December 9 1876, January 15, July 20, 25, 27, August 7, September 15, 23 1892, July 29 1893, September 18, 22, December 2, 21 1922
Sheffield Star, September 16, 18, 19, 21, 22 1922
Barnsley Times, March 10 1860, March 16 1861, April 11 1868
Barnsley Chronicle And Penistone, Mexbro', Wath, And Hoyland Journal, Saturday December 19, 26 1868
York Herald, March 15, 22 1800

The Sheffield Hanged, David Bentley, ALD Design & Print, Sheffield, 2002

The Sheffield Murders 1865–1965, David Bentley, ALD Design & Print, Sheffield, 2003

Chapter Three: Charlie Peace, The Not So Lovable Rogue and the Banner Cross Murder, 1879

The Times, November 20 1878, February 25 1879

Sheffield And Rotherham Independent, November 30, December 1, 2, 4, 5, 6, 8, 9, 11, 12, 13, 1876, 17, January 17, 18, 23, 29, 30, February 1, 2, 5, 24, 25, 26, July 5 1879

The Trials of Charles Edward Peace, Notable British Trials Series Edited by W T Shore, Wm Lodge, London, 1926

Murders and Murder Trials 1812–1912, H M Walbrook, Constable, 1938

King of the Lags The Story of Charles Peace, David Ward, Elek Books, 1963

The Romantic Career of a Great Criminal, N Kynaston, Gaskell, London, 1906

The Sheffield Murders 1865–1965, David Bentley, ALD Design & Print, Sheffield, 2003

Illustrated Police News, February 1, 8, 15, 22, March 8, 15, 29, April 5 1879

Chapter Four: The Shelf Street Hatchet Murder, 1881

Sheffield And Rotherham Independent, March 28, 29, 30, 31, April 1, May 7,10, 24 1881

Sheffield Daily Telegraph, March 28, 30 May 7, 24 1881

The Sheffield Murders 1865–1965, David Bentley, ALD Design & Print, Sheffield, 2003

Illustrated Police News, April 9 1881

Chapter Five: The Bath Street Shooting Case, 1892

Sheffield And Rotherham Independent, November 9, 10,11, 14,17 1892

Sheffield Daily Telegraph, 9, 10, 14, 17 1892

Illustrated Police News, November 18 1892

Chapter Six: Suicides, 1892

Sheffield And Rotherham Independent, February 15,16,18, 29, March 7, April 22, 29, May 9,11, June 23, July 14, 18, 19, 20, August 4, 14, 15, 19 September, 11, 14, 24 November, 20 December 1892.

Chapter Seven: The Woodhouse Murder, 1893

Sheffield And Rotherham Independent, February 17, 18, 20, 21, 23, 25, March 16, April 1, 4, 5, 6, 7 1893

Sheffield Daily Telegraph, February 17, 20, 23, 25, March 16, April 4, 5 1893

The Sheffield Murders 1865–1965, David Bentley, ALD Design & Print, Sheffield, 2003

Chapter Eight: The Walkley Murder, 1923

Sheffield Daily Independent, July 30, 31, August 4, December 8, 28, 1923

Sheffield Daily Telegraph, July 30, 31, August 1, 6, 11, December 8, 28, 29, 1923

Sheffield Star, July 31, August 6, 11, 22, 27, December 7, 8, 28, 29, 1923

The Times, July 31, December 29 1923

The Sheffield Murders 1865–1965, David Bentley, ALD Design & Print, Sheffield, 2003

Index